AUG

# FROM IMMIGRANT TO INVENTOR

## AN EXAMPLE FOR YOUNG AMERICANS

MICHAEL PUPIN

MODERN STANDARD AUTHORS

# FROM IMMIGRANT
# TO INVENTOR

## AN EXAMPLE
## FOR YOUNG AMERICANS

by

## MICHAEL PUPIN

PROFESSOR OF ELECTRO-MECHANICS
COLUMBIA UNIVERSITY

CHARLES SCRIBNER'S SONS

NEW YORK    CHICAGO    BOSTON    ATLANTA
SAN FRANCISCO            DALLAS

# PREFACE

I am happy in my belief that my publishers, Charles Scribner's Sons, are doing good service in publishing a short edition of my autobiography. I know from the many letters which I have received during the last eleven years that my autobiography is very popular among the young readers, and that there is a great demand for a short and a cheap edition of the autobiography, so as to reach a larger circle of the younger readers The autobiography was written because I believed that I had a message to deliver to the boys and girls of the United States, and to know that this message was welcome and that it will now reach a much larger circle of my young friends is very gratifying.

MICHAEL PUPIN.

NEW YORK CITY,
November, 1934.

# CONTENTS

# ILLUSTRATIONS

# I

## WHAT I BROUGHT TO AMERICA

When I landed at Castle Garden forty-eight years ago, I had only five cents in my pocket. Had I brought five hundred dollars, instead of five cents, my immediate career in the new, and to me a perfectly strange, land would have been the same. A young immigrant such as I was then does not begin his career until he has spent all the money which he has brought with him. I brought five cents, and immediately spent it upon a piece of prune pie, which turned out to be a bogus prune pie. It contained nothing but pits of prunes. If I had brought five hundred dollars, it would have taken me a little longer to spend it, mostly upon bogus things, but the struggle which awaited me would have been the same in each case. It is no handicap to a boy immigrant to land here penniless; it is not a handicap to any boy to be penniless when he strikes out for an independent career, provided that he has the stamina to stand the hardships that may be in store for him.

A thorough training in the arts and crafts and a sturdy physique capable of standing the hardships of strenuous labor do entitle the immigrant to special considerations. But what has a young and penniless immigrant to offer who has had no training in any of the arts or crafts and does not know the language of

1

the land? Apparently nothing, and if the present standards had prevailed forty-eight years ago I should have been deported. There are, however, certain things which a young immigrant may bring to this country that are far more precious than any of the things which the present immigration laws prescribe. Did I bring any of these things with me when I landed at Castle Garden in 1874? I shall try to answer this question in the following brief story of my life prior to my landing in this country.

Idvor is my native town; but the disclosure of this fact discloses very little, because Idvor cannot be found on any map. It is a little village off the highway in the province of Banat, formerly belonging to Austria-Hungary, but now an important part of the kingdom of the Serbs, Croats, and Slovenes. At the Paris peace conference, in 1919, the Rumanians claimed this province; they claimed it in vain. They could not overcome the fact that the population of Banat is Serb, and particularly of that part of Banat where Idvor is located. President Wilson and Mr. Lansing knew me personally, and when they were informed by the Yugoslav delegates in Paris that I was a native of Banat, the Rumanian arguments lost much of their plausibility. No other nationality except the Serb has ever lived in Idvor. The inhabitants of Idvor were always peasants; most of them were illiterate in my boyhood days. My father and mother could neither read nor write. The question arises now: What could a penniless boy of fifteen, born and bred under such conditions, bring to America, which under any conceivable immigration laws would entitle him to land? But I was confident that *I* was so desirable an acquisition to America that I should be allowed to land, and I was somewhat surprised that people made no fuss over me when I landed.

The Serbs of Idvor from time immemorial always considered themselves the brothers of the Serbs of Serbia, who are only a few gunshots away from Idvor on the south side of the Danube. The Avala Mountain, near Belgrade in Serbia, can easily be seen from Idvor on every clear day. This blue and, to me at that time, mysterious-looking peak seemed always like a reminder to the Serbs of Banat that the Serbs of Serbia were keeping an eye of affectionate watchfulness upon them.

When I was a boy Idvor belonged to the so-called military frontier of Austria. A bit of interesting history is attached to this name. Up to the beginning of the eighteenth century the Austrian Empire was harassed by Turkish invasions. At periodically recurring intervals Turkish armies would cross her southern frontier, formed by the Rivers Danube and Sava, and penetrate into the interior provinces. Toward the end of the seventeenth century they advanced as far as Vienna, and would have become a serious menace to the whole of Europe if the Polish king Sobiesky had not come to the rescue of Vienna. It was at that time that Emperor Leopold I, of Austria, invited Charnoyevich, the Serb Patriarch of Pech, in old Serbia, to move with thirty-five thousand picked families of old Serbia into the Austrian territory north of the Danube and the Sava Rivers, to become its guardians. For three hundred years these Serbs had been fighting the Turks and had acquired great skill in this kind of warfare. In 1690 the Patriarch with these picked families moved into Austria and settled in a narrow strip of territory on the northern banks of these two rivers. They organized what was known later as the military frontier of Austria. 1690 is, according to tradition, the date when my native village Idvor was founded, but not quite on its present site. The original site is a very small plateau a little to the north of the present site.

Banat is a perfectly level plain, but near the village of Idvor the River Tamish has dug out a miniature canyon, and on the plateau of one of the promontories of this canyon was the old site of Idvor. It is connected to the new site by a narrow neck. The old site was selected because it offered many strategical advantages of defense against the invading Turk. The first settlers of the old village lived in subterranean houses which could not be seen at a distance by the approaching enemy. Remnants of these subterranean houses were still in existence when I was a schoolboy in the village of Idvor, over fifty years ago.

The location of the original church was marked by a little column built of bricks and bearing a cross. In a recess on the side of the column was the image of St. Mary with the Christ Child, illuminated by a burning wick immersed in oil. The legend was that this flame was never allowed to go out, and that a religious procession by the good people of Idvor to the old monument was sure to avert any calamity, like pestilence or drought, that might be threatening the village. I took part in many of these processions to the old deserted village,

THE STREET ON WHICH STANDS THE PEASANT HOUSE TYPICAL OF
IDVOR, IN WHICH PUPIN WAS BORN

On the right is the spire of the church on the village green

THE OLD MONUMENT ON STARO SELO, THE OLD VILLAGE, WHERE
THE ORIGINAL SETTLERS OF IDVOR LIVED IN
SUBTERRANEAN DWELLINGS

and felt every time that I was standing upon sacred ground; sacred because of the Christian blood shed there during the struggles of the Christian Serbs of Idvor against the Turkish invaders. Every visit to the old village site refreshed the memories of the heroic traditions of which the village people were extremely proud. They were poor in worldly goods, those simple peasant folk of Idvor, but they were rich in memories of their ancient traditions.

As I look back upon my childhood days in the village of Idvor, I feel that the cultivation of old traditions was the principal element in the spiritual life of the village people. The knowledge of these traditions was necessary and sufficient to them, in order to understand their position in the world and in the Austrian Empire. When my people moved into Austria under Patriarch Charnoyevich and settled in the military frontier, they had a definite agreement with Emperor Leopold I. It was recorded in an Austrian state document called Privilegia. According to this ancient document the Serbs of the military frontier were to enjoy a spiritual, economic, and political autonomy. Lands granted to them were their own property. In our village we maintained our own schools and our own churches, and each village elected its own local administration. Its head was the Knez, or chief, usually a sturdy peasant. My father was a Knez several times. The bishops and the people elected their own spiritual and political heads, that is, the Patriarch and the Voyvoda (governor). We were free and independent peasant landlords. In return for these privileges, the people obligated themselves to render military service for the defense of the southern frontiers of the empire against the invading Turks. They had helped to drive the Turks across the Danube, under the supreme command of Prince Eugene of Savoy, in the beginning of the eighteenth century.

After the emperor had discovered the splendid fighting qualities of the Serbs of the military frontier, he managed to extend the original terms of the Privilegia so as to make it obligatory upon the military frontiersmen to defend the empire against any and every enemy. Subsequently the Serbs of the military frontier of Austria defended Empress Maria Theresa against Frederick the Great; they defended Emperor Francis against Napoleon; they defended Emperor Ferdinand against the rebellious Hungarians in 1848 and 1849; and in 1859 and 1866 they defended Austria against Italy. The military exploits of the men of Idvor during these wars supplied material for the traditions of Idvor, which were recorded in many tales and stirring songs. Reading and writing did not flourish in Idvor in those days, but poetry did.

Faithful to the old customs of the Serb race, the people of Idvor held during the long winter evenings their neighborhood gatherings, and as a boy I attended many of them at my father's house. The older men would sit around the warm stove on a bench which was a part of the stove and made of the same material, usually soft brick plastered over and whitewashed. They smoked and talked and looked like old senators, self-appointed guardians of all the wisdom of Idvor.

At the feet of the old men were middle-aged men, seated upon low stools, each with a basket in front of him, into which he peeled the yellow kernels from the seasoned ears of corn, and this kept him busy during the evening. The older women were seated on little stools along the wall; they would be spinning wool, flax, or hemp. The young women would be sewing or knitting. I, a favorite child of my mother, was allowed to sit alongside of her and listen to the words of wisdom and words of fiction dropping from the mouths of the old men and sometimes also from the mouths of middle-aged and younger men, when the old men gave them permission to speak. At intervals the young women would sing a song having some relation to the last tale. For instance, when one of the old men had finished a tale about Karageorge and his historic struggles against the Turks, the women would follow with a song describing a brave Voyvoda of Karageorge, named Hayduk Velyko, who with a small band of Serbians defended Negotin against a great Turkish army under Moula Pasha. This gallant band, as the song describes them, reminds one of the little band of Greeks at Thermopylæ.

Some of the old men present at these gatherings had taken part in the Napoleonic wars, and they remembered well also the stories which they had heard from their fathers relating to the wars of Austria against Frederick the Great during the eighteenth century. The middle-aged men had participated in the fighting during the Hungarian revolution, and the younger men had just gone through the campaigns in Italy in 1859 and 1866. One of the old men had taken part in the battle of Aspern, when Austria defeated Napoleon. He had received a high imperial decoration for bravery, and was very proud of it. He also had gone to Russia with an Austrian division during Napoleon's campaign of 1812. His name was Baba Batikin, and in the estimation of the village people he was a seer and a prophet, because of his wonderful memory and his extraordinary power of description. His diction was that of a guslar (Serbian minstrel). He not only described vividly what went on in Austria and in Russia during the Napoleonic wars in which he himself participated, but he would also thrill his hearers by tales relating to the Austrian campaigns against Frederick the Great, which his father upon his return from the battle-fields of Silesia had related to him. I remember quite well his stories relating to Karageorge of Serbia, whom he had known personally. He called him the great Vozhd, or leader of the Serbian peasants, and never grew weary of describing his heroic struggles against the Turks in the beginning of the nineteenth century. These tales about Karageorge were always received at the neighborhood gatherings with more enthusiasm than any other of his stirring narratives.

Toward the end of the evening Baba Batikin would recite some of the old Serbian ballads, many of which he knew by heart. During these recitations his thin and wrinkled face would light up; it was the face of a seer, as I remember it, and I can see now his bald head with a wonderful brow, towering over bushy eyebrows through which the light of his deep-set eyes would shine like the light of the moon through the needles of an aged pine. It was from him that the good people of Idvor learned the history of the Serb race from the battle of the field of Kossovo in 1389 down to Karageorge. He kept alive the old Serb traditions in the village of Idvor. He was my first and my best teacher in history.

The younger men told tales relating to Austrian campaigns in Italy, glorifying the deeds of valor of the men of Idvor in these campaigns. The battle of Custozza in 1866, in which the military frontiersmen nearly annihilated the Italian armies, received a great deal of attention, because the men who described it had participated in it, and had just returned from Italy. But I remember that every one of those men was full of praise of Garibaldi, the leader of the Italian people in their struggles for freedom. They called him the Karageorge of Italy.

I remember also that in my father's house, in which these winter-evening gatherings took place, there was a colored picture of Garibaldi with his red shirt and a plumed hat. The picture was hung up alongside of the Ikona, the picture of our patron saint; on the other side of the Ikona was the picture of the Czar of Russia, who only a few years before had emancipated the Russian serfs. In the same room and hanging in a very conspicuous place all by itself was a picture of Karageorge, the leader of the Serbian revolution. The picture of the Austrian emperor was not there after 1869!

The Serb ballads recited by Baba Batikin glorified the great national hero, Prince Marko, whose combats were the combats of a strong man in defense of the weak and of the oppressed. Marko, although a prince of royal blood, never fought for conquest of territory. According to the guslar, Prince Marko was a true

champion of right and justice. At that time the Civil
War in America had just come to a close, and the name
of Lincoln, whenever mentioned by Baba Batikin, suggested an American Prince Marko.

The impressions which I carried away from these
neighborhood gatherings were a spiritual food which
nourished in my young mind the sentiment that the
noblest thing in this world is the struggle for right,
justice, and freedom. It was the love of freedom and
of right and justice which made the Serbs of the
military frontier desert their ancestral homes in old
Serbia and move into Austria, where they gladly consented to live in subterranean houses and crawl like
woodchucks under the ground as long as they could
enjoy the blessings of political freedom.

The military frontiersmen had their freedom guaranteed to them by the Privilegia, and, in exchange for
their freedom, they were always ready to fight for the
Emperor of Austria on any battle-field. Loyalty to the
emperor was the cardinal virtue of the military frontiersmen. It was that loyalty which overcame their
admiration for Garibaldi in 1866; hence the Austrian
victory at Custozza. The Emperor of Austria as a
guardian of their freedom received a place of honor in
the selected class of men like Prince Marko, Karageorge, Czar Alexander the Liberator, Lincoln, and
Garibaldi. These were the names recorded in the Hall
of Fame of Idvor.

When, however, the emperor, in 1869, dissolved the
military frontier and delivered its people to the Hungarians, the military frontiersmen felt that they were

betrayed by the emperor, who had broken his faith to them recorded in the Privilegia. I remember my father saying to me one day: "Thou shalt never be a soldier in the emperor's army. The emperor has broken his word; the emperor is a traitor in the eyes of the military frontiersmen. We despise the man who is not true to his word." This is the reason why the picture of the Emperor of Austria was not allowed a place in my father's house after 1869.

As I look back upon those days I feel, as I always felt, that this treacherous act of the Austrian emperor in 1869 was the beginning of the end of the Austrian Empire. It was the beginning of nationalism in the realm of Emperor Francis Joseph of Hapsburg. The love of the people for the country in which they lived began to languish and finally died. When that love dies, the country also must die. This was the lesson which I learned from the illiterate peasants of Idvor.

My teacher in the village school never succeeded in making upon my mind that profound impression which was made upon it by the men at the neighborhood gatherings. They were men who had gone out into the world and taken an active part in the struggles of the world. Reading, writing, and arithmetic appeared to me like instruments of torture which the teacher, who, in my opinion at that time, knew nothing of the world, had invented in order to interfere as much as possible with my freedom, particularly when I had an important engagement with my chums and playmates.

But my mother soon convinced me that I was wrong. She could neither read nor write, and she told me that she always felt that she was blind, in spite of the clear vision of her eyes. So blind, indeed, that, as she expressed it, she did not dare venture into the world much beyond the confines of my native village.

This was as far as I remember now the mode of reasoning which she would address to me: "My boy, if you wish to go out into the world about which you hear so much at the neighborhood gatherings, you must provide yourself with another pair of eyes; the eyes of reading and writing. There is so much wonderful knowledge and learning in the world which you cannot get unless you can read and write. Knowledge is the golden ladder over which we climb to heaven; knowledge is the light which illuminates our path through this life and leads to a future life of everlasting glory." She was a very pious woman, and had a rare knowledge of both the Old and the New Testaments. The Psalms were her favorite recitations. She knew also the lives of saints. St. Sava was her favorite saint. She was the first to make me understand the story of the life of this wonderful Serb.

This, briefly stated, was the story which she told me: Sava was the youngest son of the Serb Zhupan Nemanya. At an early age he renounced his royal titles and retired to a monastery on Mount Athos and devoted many years to study and meditation. He then returned to his native land, in the beginning of the thirteenth century, and became the first Serbian archbishop and founded an autonomous Serbian church. He also organized public schools in his father's realm, where Serbian boys and girls had an opportunity to learn how to read and write. Thus he opened the eyes of the Serbian people, and the people in grateful recognition of these great services called him St. Sava the Educator, and praised forever his saintly name and memory. Seven hundred years had passed since St. Sava's time, but not one of them had passed without a memorial celebration dedicated to him in every town and in every home where a Serb lived.

This was a revelation to me. Like every schoolboy, I attended, of course, every year in January, the celebrations of St. Sava's day. On these occasions we unruly boys made fun of the big boy who in a trembling and awkward voice was reciting something about St. Sava, which the teacher had written out for him. After this recitation, the teacher, with a funny nasal twang, would do his best to supplement in a badly articulated speech what he had written out for the big boy, and finally the drowsy-looking priest would wind up with a sermon bristling with archaic Slavonic church expressions, which to us unruly boys sounded like awkward attempts of a Slovak mouse-trap dealer to speak Serbian. Our giggling merriment then reached a climax, and so my mischievous chums never gave me a chance to catch the real meaning of the ceremonies on St. Sava's day.

My mother's story of St. Sava and the way in which she told it made the image of St. Sava appear before me for the first time in the light of a saint who glorified the value of books and of the art of writing. I understood then why mother placed such value upon reading and writing. I vowed to devote myself to both, even if that should make it necessary to neglect my chums and playmates, and soon I convinced my mother that in reading and writing I could do at least as well as any boy.

The teacher observed the change; he was astonished, and actually believed that a miracle had occurred. My mother believed in miracles, and told the teacher that the spirit of St. Sava was guiding me. One day she told him in my presence that in a dream she saw St. Sava lay his hands upon my head, and then turning to her say: "Daughter Piada, your boy will soon outgrow the village school of Idvor. Let him then go out into the world, where he can find more brain food for his hungry head."

Next year the teacher selected me to make the recitation on St. Sava's day, and he wrote out the speech for me. My mother amended and amplified it and made me rehearse it for her over and over again. On St. Sava's day the first public speech of my life was delivered by me. The success was overwhelming. My chums, the unruly boys, did not giggle; on the contrary, they looked interested, and that encouraged me much. The people said to each other that even old Baba Batikin could not have done much better. My mother cried for joy; my teacher shook his head, and the priest looked puzzled, and they both admitted that I had outgrown the village school of Idvor.

At the end of that year my mother prevailed upon my father to send me to a higher school in the town of Panchevo, on the Tamish River, about fifteen miles south of Idvor, quite near the point where the Tamish flows into the Danube. There I found teachers whose learning made a deep impression upon me, particularly their learning in natural science, a subject entirely unknown in Idvor. There I heard for the first time that an American named Franklin, operating with a kite and a key, had discovered that lightning was a passage of an electrical spark between clouds, and that thunder was due to the sudden expansion of the atmosphere heated by the passage of the electrical spark. The story was illustrated by an actual frictional electrical machine. This information thrilled me; it was so novel and so simple, I thought, and so contrary to all my previous notions.

During my visit home I eagerly took the first opportunity to describe this new knowledge to my father and his peasant friends, who were seated in front of our house and were enjoying their Sunday-afternoon talks. I suddenly observed that my father and his friends looked at each other in utter astonishment. They seemed to ask each other the question: "What heresy may this be which this impudent brat is disclosing to us?" And then my father, glaring at me, asked whether I had forgotten that he had told me on so many occasions that thunder was due to the rumbling of St. Elijah's car as he drove across the heavens, and whether I thought that this American Franklin, who played with kites like an idle boy, knew more than the wisest men of Idvor.

I always had a great respect for my father's opinions, but on that occasion I could not help smiling with a smile of ill-concealed irony which angered him. When I saw the flame of anger in his big black eyes I jumped and ran for safety. During supper my father, whose anger had cooled considerably, described to my mother the heresy which I was preaching on that afternoon. My mother observed that nowhere in the Holy Scriptures could he find support of the St. Elijah legend, and that it was quite possible that the American Franklin was right and that the St. Elijah legend was wrong. In matters of correct interpretation of ancient authorities my father was always ready to abide by the decisions of my mother, and so father and I became reconciled again. My mother's admission of the possibility that the American Franklin might, after all, be wiser than all the wise men of Idvor, and my father's silent consent, aroused in me a keen interest in America. Lincoln and Franklin were two names with which my early ideas of America were associated.

During those school-days in Panchevo I passed my summer vacation in my native village. Idvor, just like the rest of Banat, lives principally from agriculture, and during harvest-time it is as busy as a beehive. Old and young, man and beast, concentrate all their efforts upon the harvest operations. But nobody is busier than the Serbian ox. He is the most loyal and effective servant of the Serb peasant everywhere, and particularly in Banat. He does all the ploughing in the spring, and he hauls the seasoned grain from the distant fertile fields to the threshing-grounds in the village when the harvesting season is on. The commencement of the threshing operations marks the end of the strenuous efforts of the good old ox; his summer vacation begins, and he is sent to pasture-lands to feed and to rest and to prepare himself for autumn hauling of the yellow corn and for the autumn ploughing of the fields. The village boys who are not big enough to

THE HOUSE IN WHICH MICHAEL PUPIN WAS BORN, AT IDVOR

render much help on the threshing-grounds are assigned to the task of watching over the grazing oxen during their summer vacation. The school vacation of the boys coincided with the vacation of the good old ox. Several summers I passed in that interesting occupation. These were my only summer schools, and they were the most interesting schools that I ever attended.

The oxen of the village were divided into herds of about fifty head, and each herd was guarded by a squad of some twelve boys from families owning the oxen in the herd. Each squad was under the command of a young man who was an experienced herdsman. To watch a herd of fifty oxen was not an easy task. In daytime the job was easy, because the heat of the summer sun and the torments of the ever-busy fly made the oxen hug the shade of the trees, where they rested awaiting the cooler hours of the day. At night, however, the task was much more difficult. Being forced to hug the shade of the trees during daytime, the oxen would get but little enjoyment of the pasture, and so when the night arrived they were quite hungry and eagerly searched for the best of feed.

I must mention now that the pasture-lands of my native village lay alongside of territory of a score of square miles which in some years were all planted in corn. During the months of August and September these vast corn-fields were like deep forests. Not far from Idvor and to the east of the corn-fields was a Rumanian settlement which was notorious for its cattle-thieves. The trick of these thieves was to hide in the corn-fields at night and to wait until some cattle strayed into these fields, when they would drive them away and hide them somewhere in their own corn-fields on the other side of their own village. To prevent the herd from straying into the corn-fields at night was a great task, for the performance of which the boys had to be trained in daytime by their experienced leader.

It goes without saying that each day we boys first worked off our superfluous energy in wrestling, swimming, hockey, and other strenuous games, and then settled down to the training in the arts of a herdsman which we had to practise at night. One of these arts was signalling through the ground. Each boy had a knife with a long wooden handle. This knife was stuck deep into the ground. A sound was made by striking against the wooden handle, and the boys, lying down and pressing their ears close to the ground, had to estimate the direction and the distance of the origin of sound. Practice made us quite expert in this form of signalling. We knew at that time that the sound travelled through the ground far better than through the air, and that a hard and solid ground transmitted sound much better than the ploughed-up ground. We knew, therefore, that the sound produced this way near the edge of the pasture-land could not be heard in the soft ground of the corn-fields stretching along the edge. A Rumanian cattle-thief, hidden at night in the corn-fields, could not hear our ground signals and could not locate us. Kos, the Slovenian, my teacher and interpreter of physical phenomena, could not explain this, and I doubt very much whether the average physicist of Europe at that time could have explained it. It is the basis of a discovery which I made about twenty-five years after my novel experiences in that herdsmen's summer school in Idvor.

On perfectly clear and quiescent summer nights on the plains of my native Banat, the stars are intensely bright and the sky looks black by contrast. "Thy hair is as black as the sky of a summer midnight" is a favorite saying of a Serbian lover to his lady-love. On such nights we could not see our grazing oxen when they were more than a few score of feet from us, but we could hear them if we pressed our ears close to the ground and listened. On such nights we boys had our work cut out for us. We were placed along a definite line at distances of some twenty yards apart.

This was the dead-line, which separated the pasture-lands from the corn-field territory. The motto of the French at Verdun was: "They shall not pass!" This was our motto, too, and it referred equally to our friends, the oxen, and to our enemies, the Rumanian cattle-thieves. Our knife-blades were deep in the ground and our ears were pressed against the handles. We could hear every step of the roaming oxen and even their grazing operations when they were sufficiently near to the dead-line. We knew that these grazing operations were regulated by the time of the night, and this we estimated by the position of certain constellations like Orion and the Pleiades.

The positions of the evening star and of the morning star also were closely observed. Venus was our white star and Mars was called the red star. The Dipper, the north star, and the milky way were our compass. We knew also that when in the dead of the night we could hear the faint sound of the church-bell of the Rumanian settlement about four miles to the east of us, then there was a breeze from the corn-fields to the pasture-lands, and that it carried the sweet perfume of the young corn to the hungry oxen, inviting them to the rich banquet-table of the corn-fields. On such nights our vigilance was redoubled. We were then all eyes and ears. Our ears were closely pressed to the ground and our eyes were riveted upon the stars above.

The light of the stars, the sound of the grazing oxen, and the faint strokes of the distant church-bell were messages of caution which on those dark summer nights guided our vigilance over the precious herd. These messages appealed to us like the loving words of a friendly power, without whose aid we were helpless. They were the only signs of the world's existence which dominated our consciousness as, enveloped in the darkness of night and surrounded by countless burning stars, we guarded the safety of our oxen. The rest of the world had gone out of existence; it began to reappear in our consciousness when the early dawn announced what we boys felt to be the divine command, "Let there be light," and the sun heralded by long white streamers began to approach the eastern sky, and the earth gradually appeared as if by an act of creation. Every one of those mornings of fifty years ago appeared to us herdsmen to be witnessing the creation of the world—a world at first of friendly sound and light messages which made us boys feel that a divine power was protecting us and our herd, and then a real terrestrial world, when the rising sun had separated the hostile mysteries of night from the friendly realities of the day.

Sound and light became thus associated in my early modes of thought with the divine method of speech and communication, and this belief was strengthened by my mother, who quoted the words of St. John: "In the beginning was the word, and the word was with God, and the word was God."

I believed also that David, some of whose Psalms, under the instruction of my mother, I knew by heart, and who in his youth was a shepherd, expressed my thoughts in his nineteenth Psalm:

"The heavens declare the glory of God. . . ."

. . . . . . . . . .

"There is no speech nor language, where their voice is not heard."

Then, there is no Serb boy who has not heard that beautiful Russian song by Lyermontoff, the great Russian poet, which says:

"Lonely I wander over the country road,
And in the darkness the stony path is glimmering;
Night is silent and the plains are whispering
To God, and star speaketh to star."

Lyermontoff was a son of the Russian plains. He saw the same burning stars in the blackness of a summer midnight sky which I saw. He felt the same thrill which David felt and through his Psalms transmitted to me during those watchful nights of fifty years ago.

I pity the city-bred boy who has never felt the mysterious force of that heavenly thrill.

Sound and light being associated in my young mind of fifty years ago with divine operations by means of which man communicates with man, beast with beast, stars with stars, and man with his Creator, it is obvious that I meditated much about the nature of sound and of light. I still believe that these modes of communication are the fundamental operations in the physical universe and I am still meditating about their nature. My teachers in Panchevo rendered some assistance in solving many of the puzzles which I met in the course of these meditations. Kos, my Slovenian teacher, who was the first to tell me the story of Franklin and his kite, was a great help. He soon convinced me that sound was a vibration of bodies. This explanation agreed with the Serbian figure of speech which says:

"My heart quivers like the melodious string under the guslar's bow."

I also felt the quivering air whenever during my term of service as guardian of the oxen I tried my skill at the Serbian flute. Few things excited my interest more than the operations of the Serbian bagpiper as he forced the air from his sheepskin bellows and made it sing by regulating its passage through the pipes. The operations which the bagpiper called adjustment and tuning of the bagpipes commanded my closest attention. I never dreamed then that a score of years later I should do a similar operation with an electrical circuit. I called it "electrical tuning," a term which has been generally adopted in wireless telegraphy.

But nobody knows that the operation as well as the name were first suggested to me by the Serbian bagpiper, some twenty years before I made the invention in 1892.

Skipping over several sections of my story, I will say now that twenty years after my invention of electrical tuning a pupil of mine, Major Armstrong, discovered the electrical vacuum-tube oscillator, which promises to revolutionize wireless telegraphy and telephony. A similar invention, but a little earlier, was made by another pupil of mine, Mr. Vreeland. Both these inventions in their mode of operation remind me much of the operation of Serbian bagpipes. Perhaps some of those thrills which the Serbian bagpiper stirred up in me in my early youth were transferred to my pupils, Armstrong and Vreeland.

I was less successful in solving my puzzles concerning the nature of light. Kos, the Slovenian, my first guide and teacher in the study of physical phenomena, told me the story that a wise man of Greece with the name of Aristotle believed that light originates in the eye, which throws out feelers to the surrounding objects, and that through these feelers we see the objects, just as we feel them by our sense of touch. This view did not agree with the popular saying often heard in Idvor: "Pick your grapes before sunrise, before the thirsty sunbeams have drunk up their cooling dew." Nor did it agree with Bishop Nyegosh, the greatest of Serbian poets, who says:

"The bright-eyed dewdrops glide along the sunbeams to the heavens above."

The verse from Nyegosh I obtained from a Serbian poet, who was an arch-priest, a protoyeray, and who was my religious teacher in Panchevo. His name, Vasa Zhivkovich, I shall never forget, because it is sweet music to my ears on account of the memories of affectionate friendship he cherished for me.

According to this popular belief a beam of light has an individual existence just like that of the melodious string under the guslar's bow. But neither the poet, nor the wise men of Idvor, nor Kos the Slovenian, ever mentioned that a beam of light ever quivered, and if it does not quiver like a vibrating body how can the sun, the moon, and the stars proclaim the glory of God, and how can, according to David, their voice be heard wherever there are speech and language? These questions Kos would not answer. No wonder! Nobody today can give a completely satisfactory answer to questions relating to radiation of light. Kos was non-committal and did not seem to attach much importance to the authorities which I quoted; namely, the Serbian poet Nyegosh, the wise sayings of Idvor, and the Psalms of David. Nevertheless, he was greatly interested in my childlike inquiries and always encouraged me to go on with my puzzling questions. Once he invited me to his house, and there I found that several of his colleagues were present. One of them was my friend the poet-priest, and another was a Hungarian Lutheran preacher who spoke Serbian well and was famous in Panchevo because of his great eloquence.

They both engaged me in conversation and showed a lively interest in my summer vacation experiences

as herdsman's assistant. The puzzling questions about
light which I addressed to Kos, and the fact that Kos
would not answer, amused them. My knowledge of the
Bible and of the Psalms impressed them much, and
they asked me quite a number of questions concerning
my mother. Then they suggested that I might be
transferred from the school in Panchevo to the famous
schools of Prague in Bohemia, if my father and mother
did not object to my going so far away from home.
When I suggested that my parents could not afford
to support me in a great place like Prague, they assured
me that this difficulty might be fixed up. I promised
to consult my parents during the approaching Christ-
mas vacation. I did, but found my father irresistibly
opposed to it. Fate, however, decreed otherwise.

The history of Banat records a great event for the
early spring of 1872, the spring succeeding the Christ-
mas when my father and mother agreed to disagree
upon the proposition that I go to Prague. Svetozar
Miletich, the great nationalist leader of the Serbs in
Austria-Hungary, visited Panchevo, and the people
prepared a torchlight procession for him. This procession was to be a protest of Panchevo and of the whole
of Banat against the emperor's treachery of 1869. My
father had protested long before by excluding the
emperor's picture from our house.

That visit of Miletich marks the beginning of a new
political era in Banat, the era of nationalism. The
schoolboys of Panchevo turned out in great numbers,
and I was one of them, proud to become one of the
torch-bearers. We shouted ourselves hoarse whenever
Miletich in his fiery speech denounced the emperor

for his ingratitude to the military frontiersmen as well as to all the Serbs of Voyvodina. Remembering my father's words on the occasion mentioned above, I did not hesitate to shout in the name of the schoolboys present in the procession: "We'll never serve in Francis Joseph's army!" My chums responded with: "Long live the Prince of Serbia!" The Hungarian officials took careful notes of the whole proceeding, and a few days later I was informed that Panchevo was not a proper place for an ill-mannered peasant boy like me, and that I should pack up and return to Idvor. Kos, the Slovenian, and protoyeray Zhivkovich interfered, and I was permitted to stay.

On the first of May, following, our school celebrated the May-day festival. The Serb youngsters in the school, who worshipped Miletich and his nationalism, prepared a Serbian flag for the festival march. The other boys, mostly Germans, Rumanians, and Hungarians, carried the Austrian yellow-black standard. The nationalist group among the youngsters stormed the bearer of the yellow-black standard, and I was caught in the scrimmage with the Austrian flag under my feet. Expulsion from school stared me in the face. Again protoyeray Zhivkovich came to my defense and, thanks to his high official position and to my high standing in school, I was allowed to continue with my class until the end of the school year, after promising that I would not associate with revolutionary boys who showed an inclination to storm the Austrian flag. The matter did not end there, however. In response to an invitation from the protoyeray, father and mother came to Panchevo to a conference, which resulted in a triumph for my mother. It was decided that I bid good-by to Panchevo, a hotbed of nationalism, and go to Prague. The protoyeray and his congregation promised assistance if the financial burden attached to my schooling in Prague should prove too heavy for my parents.

When the day for the departure for Prague arrived, my mother had everything ready for my long journey, a journey of nearly two days on a Danube steamboat to Budapest, and one day by rail from Budapest to Prague. Two multicolored bags made of a beautifully colored web of wool contained my belongings; one my linen, the other my provisions, consisting of a whole roast goose and a big loaf of white bread. The only suit of clothes which I had I wore on my back, and my sisters told me that it was very stylish and made me look like a city-bred boy. To tone down somewhat this misleading appearance and to provide a warm covering during my journey for the cold autumn evenings and nights, I wore a long yellow overcoat of sheepskin trimmed with black wool and embroidered along the border with black and red arabesque figures. A black sheepskin cap gave the finishing touch and marked me as a real son of Idvor.

When I said good-by to father and mother on the steamboat landing I expected, of course, that my mother would cry, and she did; but to my great surprise I noticed two big tears roll down my father's cheeks. He was a stern and unemotional person, a splendid type of the heroic age, and when for the first time in my life I saw a tear in his luminous eyes I broke down and sobbed, and felt embarrassed when I saw that the steamboat passengers were taking a sympathetic interest in my parting from father and mother. A group of big boys on the boat took me up and offered to help me to orient myself on the boat; they were theological students returning to the famous seminary at Karlovci, the seat of the Serb Patriarch. I confided to them that I was going to the schools of Prague, that I never had gone from home farther than Panchevo, that I had never seen a big steamboat or a railroad-train, and that my journey gave me some anxiety because I could not speak Hungarian and had some difficulty in handling the limited German vocabulary which I learned in Panchevo.

Presently we saw a great church-tower in the distance, and they told me that it was the cathedral of Karlovci, and that near the cathedral was the palace of his holiness, the Patriarch. It was at this place that the Turks begged for peace in 1699, having been defeated with the aid of the military frontiersmen. Beyond Karlovci, they pointed out, was the mountain of Frushka Gora, famous in Serbian poetry. This was the first time I saw a mountain at close range. One historical scene crowded upon another, and I had some difficulty to take them all in, even with the friendly assistance of my theological acquaintances. When Karlovci was reached and my theological friends left the boat, I felt quite lonesome. I returned to my multicolored bags, and as I looked upon them and remembered that mother had made them I felt that a part, at least, of my honey-hearted home was so near me, and that consoled me.

I noticed that lunch was being served to people who had ordered it, and I thought of the roast goose which mother had packed away in my multicolored bag. I reached for the bag, but, alas! the goose was gone. A fellow passenger, who sat near me, assured me that he saw one of the young theologians carry the goose away while the other theologians engaged me in conversation, and not knowing to whom the bags belonged, he thought nothing of the incident. Besides, how could any one suspect a student of theology? "Shades of St. Sava," said I, "what kind of orthodoxy will these future apostles of your faith preach to the Serbs of Banat?" "Ah, my boy," said an elderly lady who heard my exclamation, "do not curse them; they did it just out of innocent mischief. This experience will be worth many a roast goose to you; it will teach you that in a world of strangers you must always keep one eye on what you have and with the other eye look out for things that you do not have." She was a most sympathetic peasant woman, who probably had seen my dramatic parting with father and mother on the steamboat landing. I took her advice, and during the rest of my journey I never lost sight of my multicolored bags and of my yellow sheepskin coat.

The sight of Budapest, as the boat approached it on the following day, nearly took my breath away. At the neighborhood gatherings in Idvor I had heard many a story about the splendor of the emperor's palace on

the top of the mountain at Buda, and about the
wonders of a bridge suspended in air across the Danube
and connecting Buda with Pest. Many legends were
told in Idvor concerning these wonderful things. But
what I saw with my own eyes from the deck of that
steamboat surpassed all my expectations. I was overawed, and for a moment I should have been glad to
turn back and retrace my journey to Idvor. The world
outside of Idvor seemed too big and too complicated
for me.

But as soon as I landed my courage returned. With
the yellow sheepskin coat on my back, the black sheepskin cap on my head, and the multicolored bags firmly
grasped in my hands, I started out to find the railroad-
station. A husky Serb passed by and, attracted by my
sheepskin coat and cap and the multicolored bags,
suddenly stopped and addressed me in Serbian. He
lived in Budapest, he said, and his glad eye and hand
assured me that a sincere friend was speaking to me.
He helped me with the bags and stayed with me until
he deposited me in the train that was to take me to
Prague. He cautioned me that at about four o'clock
in the morning my train would reach Gaenserndorf
(Goosetown), and that there I should get out and get
another train which would take me to Prague. The
name of this town brought back to memory my goose
which had disappeared at Karlovci, and gloomy fore-
bodings disturbed my mind and made me a little
anxious.

This was the first railroad-train that I had ever seen.
It disappointed me; the legendary speed of trains

about which I had heard so much in Idvor was not there. When the whistle blew and the conductor shouted "Fertig!" (Ready!), I shut my eyes and waited anxiously, expecting to be shot forward at a tremendous speed. But the train started leisurely and, to my great disappointment, never reached the speeds which I expected. It was a cold October night; the third-class compartment had only one other passenger, a fat Hungarian whom I could not understand, although he tried his best to engage me in a conversation. My sheepskin coat and cap made me feel warm and comfortable; I fell asleep, and never woke up until the rough conductor pulled me off my seat and ordered me out.

"Vienna, last stop," he shouted.

"But I was going to Prague," I said.

"Then you should have changed at Gaenserndorf, you idiot!" answered the conductor, with the usual politeness of Austrian officials when they see a Serb before them. "But why didn't you wake me up at Gaenserndorf?" I protested. He flared up and made a gesture as if about to box my ears, but suddenly he changed his mind and substituted a verbal thrust at my pride. "You little fool of a Serbian swineherd, do you expect an imperial official to assist you in your lazy habits, you sleepy muttonhead?"

"Excuse me," I said with an air of wounded pride, "I am not a Serbian swineherd; I am a son of a brave military frontiersman, and I am going to the famous schools of Prague."

He softened, and told me that I should have to go back to Gaenserndorf after paying my fare to that place and back. When I informed him that I had no money for extra travelling expenses, he beckoned to me to come along, and after a while we stood in the presence of what I thought to be a very great official. He had a lot of gold braid on his collar and sleeves and on his cap, and he looked as stern and as serious as if the cares of the whole empire rested upon his shoulders.

"Take off your cap, you ill-mannered peasant! Don't you know how to behave in the presence of your superiors?" he blurted out, addressing me. I dropped my multicolored bags, took off my yellow sheepskin coat in order to cover the bags, and then took off my black sheepskin cap, and saluted him in the regular fashion of a military frontiersman. I thought that he might be the emperor himself and, if so, I wondered if he had ever heard of my trampling upon his yellow-black flag at that May-day festival in Panchevo. Finally, I screwed up my courage and apologized by saying:

"Your gracious Majesty will pardon my apparent lack of respect to my superiors, but this is to me a world of strangers, and the anxiety about my belongings kept my hands busy with the bags and prevented me from taking off my cap when I approached your serene Highness." I noticed that several persons within hearing distance were somewhat amused by this interview, and particularly an elderly looking couple, a lady and a gentleman:

"Why should you feel anxious about your bags?" said the great official. "You are not in the savage Balkans, the home of thieves; you are in Vienna, the residence of his Majesty, the Emperor of Austria-Hungary."

"Yes," said I, "but two days ago my roast goose was stolen from one of these bags within his Majesty's realm, and my father told me that all the rights and privileges of the Voyvodina and of the military frontier were stolen right here in this very Vienna."

"Ah, you little rebel, do you expect that this sort of talk will get you a free transportation from Gaenserndorf to Vienna and back again? Restrain your rebellious tongue or I will give you a free transportation back to your military frontier, where rebels like you ought to be behind lock and key."

At this juncture the elderly looking couple engaged him in conversation, and after a while the gold-braided mogul informed me that my ticket from Vienna to Prague by the short route was paid for, and that I should proceed. The rude conductor, who had called me a Serbian swineherd a little while before, led me to the train and ushered me politely into a first-class compartment. Presently the elderly looking couple entered and greeted me in a most friendly, almost affectionate manner. They encouraged me to take off my sheepskin coat and make myself comfortable, and assured me that my bags would be perfectly safe.

Their German speech had a strange accent, and their manner and appearance were entirely different from anything that I had ever seen before. But they inspired confidence. Feeling hungry, I took my loaf of snowy-white bread out of my bag, and with my herdsman's knife with a long wooden handle I cut off two slices and offered them to my new friends. "Please, take it," said I; "it was prepared by my mother's hands for my long journey." They accepted my hospitality and ate the bread and pronounced it excellent, the best bread they had ever tasted. I told them how it was made by mixing leaf-lard and milk with the finest wheat flour, and when I informed them that I knew a great deal about cooking and that I had learned it by watching my mother, the lady appeared greatly pleased.

The gentleman, her husband, asked me questions about farming and taking care of animals, which I answered readily, quoting my father as my authority. "You had two splendid teachers, your father and your mother," they said; "do you expect to find better teachers in Prague?" I told them briefly what had sent me to Prague, mentioning particularly that some people thought that I had outgrown the schools not only of my native village but also of Panchevo, but that in reality the main reason was because the Hungarian officials did not want me in Panchevo on account of my showing a strong inclination to develop into a rebellious nationalist. My new friends gave each other a significant look and said something in a language which I did not understand. They told me that it was English, and added that they were from America.

"America!" said I, quivering with emotion. "Then you must know a lot about Benjamin Franklin and his kite, and about Lincoln, the American Prince Marko."

This exclamation of mine surprised them greatly and furnished the topic for a lively conversation of several hours, until the train had reached Prague. It was conducted in broken German, but we understood

each other perfectly. I told them of my experience
with Franklin's theory of lightning, and of its clash
with my father's St. Elijah legend, and answered many
of their questions relating to my calling Lincoln an
American Prince Marko. I quoted from several Serbian
ballads relating to Prince Marko which I had learned
from Baba Batikin, and at their urgent request described with much detail the neighborhood gatherings
in Idvor. They returned the compliment by telling me
stories of Benjamin Franklin, of Lincoln, and of America, and urged me to read "Uncle Tom's Cabin," a
translation of which I discovered some time afterward.
When the train reached Prague they insisted that I be
their guest at their Prague hotel, called the Blue Star,
for a day, at least, until I found my friends in Prague.
I gladly accepted, and spent a delightful evening with
them. The sweetness of their disposition was an un-
fathomable riddle to me. The riddle, however, was
solved several years later.

I mentioned above that the first sight of Budapest
nearly took my breath away. The first view of Prague
filled me with a strange religious fervor. The ancient
gates, surmounted by towers with wonderful stone
carvings and inscriptions; the lofty domes, crowning
mediæval cathedrals, the portals of which were bristling with beautiful images of saints; the historic public
buildings, each of which told a story of the old glories
of Bohemia's kingdom; the ancient stone bridge across
the Moldava River, supporting statues of Christian
martyrs; the royal palace on the hill of Hradchin,
which seemed to rise way up above the clouds—all

these, and many other wonderful things, made me feel that it was places like Prague which St. Sava visited when he deserted his royal parents and went to the end of the world to seek new knowledge. I saw then why the protoyeray of Panchevo had suggested that I go to Prague; I even began to suspect that he expected the influence of Prague to turn my attention to theology. I think now that it would have done so if it had not been for that unpleasant goose incident at Karlovci. Besides, there was another influence at Prague, which was more powerful than any other influence in the Austrian Empire at that time.

The sights of Prague interested me more than its famous schools, which I was to enter and delayed entering. But finally I was enrolled, and the boys in the school scrutinized me with a puzzled expression, as if they could not make out what country or clime I came from. When they found out that I hailed from the Serb military frontier, all uncertainty vanished, and I knew exactly where I stood. The German boys became very cold, the Czech boys greeted me in their own tongue and hugged me when by my Serbian answer I proved not only that I understood them but also that I expected them to understand my Serbian greeting. They were all nationalists to the core and did their best to make me join their ranks, which, after some reluctance, I finally did. I showed them then two letters from protoyeray Zhivkovich introducing me to Rieger and to Palacky, the great apostles of Panslavism and of nationalism in Bohemia. From that day on I was one of their young revolutionary set, and henceforth school lessons looked tame and lost most of their charm to me.

The German victory in France two years prior to that time, resulting as it did in the creation of a united Germany, had encouraged Teutonism to run riot wherever it met a current opposing it, as it did in Prague. Nationalism in Bohemia was a reaction against Austrian Teutonism in those days, just as it was a reaction against Magyarism in Voyvodina and in the military frontier. Hardly a day passed without serious clashes between the Czech nationalist boys and their German classmates. That which made my stay in Panchevo impossible met me in Prague in an even more violent form. Loyal to the traditions of the Serbian military frontiersmen, I liked nothing better than a good fight, and I had the physique and the practice, gained in the pasturelands of Idvor, to lick any German boy of my age or even older. The German pupils feared me, and the German teachers condemned what they called my revolutionary tendencies, and threatened to send me back to Idvor.

As time went on, I began to wish that they would expel me and give me a good excuse to return to Idvor. I missed the wide horizon of the plains of Banat in the narrow streets of Prague. My little bedroom in a garret, the only living quarters that I could afford, was a sad contrast to my mode of life on the endless plains of Banat, where for six weeks each summer I had lived under the wide canopy of heaven, watching the grazing oxen, gazing upon the countless stars at night, and listening to the sweet strains of the Serbian flute. The people I met on the streets were puffed up with Teutonic pride or with official arrogance; they had none of the gentle manliness and friendliness of the military frontiersmen. The teachers looked to me more like Austrian gendarmes than like sympathetic friends. They cared more for my sentiments toward the emperor and for my ideas about nationalism than for my ideas relating to God and his beautiful world of life and light. Not one of them reminded me of Kos, the Slovenian, or of protoyeray Zhivkovich in Panchevo. Race antagonism was at that time the ruling passion. If it had not been for the affectionate regard which the Czech boys and their parents had for me I should have felt most lonesome; from Banat to Prague was too sudden a change for me.

Another circumstance I must mention now which helped to brace me up. I delivered, after many months of delay, my letters of introduction to Rieger and to Palacky. I saw their pictures, I read about them, and finally I heard them address huge nationalist meetings. They were great men, I thought, and I could not screw up sufficient courage to call on them, as the protoyeray wished me to do, and waste their precious time on my account. But when I received a letter from the protoyeray in Panchevo asking why I had not delivered the letters of introduction he had given me, I made the calls. Rieger looked like my father: dark, stern, reserved, powerful of physique, with a wonderful luminosity in his eyes. He gave me coffee and cake, consuming a generous supply of them himself. When I kissed his hand, bidding him good-by, he gave me a florin for pocket-money, patted me on the cheek, and assured me that I could easily come up to the protoyeray's expectations and surprise my teachers if I would only spend more time on my books and less on my nationalist chums. This suggestion and indirect advice made me very thoughtful.

Palacky was a gentle, smooth-faced, old gentleman, who looked to me then as if he knew everything that men had ever known, and that much study had made him pale and delicate. He was much interested in my description of the life and customs of my native village, and when I mentioned St. Sava, he drew a parallel between this saint and Yan Huss, the great Czech patriot and divine, who was burned at the stake in 1415 at Constance because he demanded a national democratic church in Bohemia. He gave me a book in which I could read all about Huss and the Hussite wars and about the one-eyed Zhizhka, the great Hussite general. He gave me no coffee nor cake, probably because his health did not permit him to indulge in eatables between meals, but assured me of assistance if I should ever need it. I eagerly read the book about Yan Huss and the Hussite wars, and became a more enthusiastic nationalist than ever before. I felt that Rieger's influence pulled me in one direction, and that Palacky encouraged me to persist in the opposite direction which I had selected under the influence of the spirit of Czech nationalism.

In my letters to my elder sisters, which they read to father and mother, I described with much detail the beauties and wonders of Prague, my receptions and

talks with Rieger and Palacky, and elaborated much
the parallel between St. Sava and Yan Huss to which
Palacky had drawn my attention, and which I expected
would please my mother; but I never mentioned
Rieger's advice that I stick to books and leave the nationalist propaganda of the boys alone. I never during
my whole year's stay in Prague sent a report home on
my school work, because I never did more than just
enough to prevent my dropping to the lower grade.
My mother and the protoyeray in Panchevo expected
immeasurably more. Hence, I never complained about
the smallness of the allowance which my parents could
give me, and, therefore, they did not appeal to my
Panchevo friends for the additional help which they
had promised. I felt that I had no right to make such
an appeal, because I did not devote myself entirely to
the work for which I was sent to Prague.

While debating with myself whether to follow Rieger's advice and leave nationalism in the hands of more
experienced people and devote myself to my lessons
only, an event occurred which was the turning-point
in my life. I received a letter from my sister informing
me that my father had died suddenly after a very brief
illness. She told me also that my father had had a
premonition that he would die soon and never see me
again when, a year before, he bade me good-by on the
steamboat landing. I understood then the meaning of
the tears which on that day of parting I had seen roll
down his cheeks for the first time in my life. I immediately informed my mother that I wanted to return
to Idvor and help her take care of my father's land.

But she would not listen, and insisted that I stay in Prague, where I was seeing and learning so many wonderful things. I knew quite well what a heavy burden my schooling would be to her, and my school record did not entitle me to expect the protoyeray to make his promise of assistance good. I decided to find a way of relieving my mother of any further burdens so far as I was concerned.

One day I saw on the last page of an illustrated paper an advertisement of the Hamburg-American line, offering steerage transportation from Hamburg to New York for twenty-eight florins. I thought of my mellow-hearted American friends of the year before who bought a first-class railroad-ticket for me from Vienna to Prague, and decided on the spot to try my fortune in the land of Franklin and Lincoln as soon as I could save up and otherwise scrape up money enough to carry me from Prague to New York. My books, my watch, my clothes, including the yellow sheepskin coat and the black sheepskin cap, were all sold to make up the sum necessary for travelling expenses. I started out with just one suit of clothes on my back and a few changes of linen, and a red Turkish fez which nobody would buy. And why should anybody going to New York bother about warm clothes? Was not New York much farther south than Panchevo, and does not America suggest a hot climate when one thinks of the pictures of naked Indians so often seen? These thoughts consoled me when I parted with my sheepskin coat.

At length I came to Hamburg, ready to embark but with no money to buy a mattress and a blanket for my bunk in the steerage. Several days later my ship, the *Westphalia,* sailed—on the twelfth day of March, 1874. My mother received several days later my letter, mailed in Hamburg, telling her in most affectionate terms that, in my opinion, I had outgrown the school, the teachers, and the educational methods of Prague, and was about to depart for the land of Franklin and Lincoln, where the wisdom of people was beyond anything that even St. Sava had ever known. I assured her that with her blessing and God's help I should certainly succeed, and promised that I would soon return rich in rare knowledge and in honors. The letter was dictated by the rosiest optimism that I could invent. Several months later I found to my great delight that my mother had accepted cheerfully this rosy view of my unexpected enterprise.

The ship sailed with a full complement of steerage passengers, mostly Germans. As we glided along the River Elbe the emigrants were all on deck, watching the land as it gradually vanished from our sight. Presently the famous German emigrant song rang through the air, and with a heavy heart I took in the words of its refrain:

"Oh, how hard it would be to leave the homeland shores
If the hope did not live that soon we shall see them again.
Farewell, farewell, until we see you again."

I did not wait for the completion of the song, but turned in, and in my bare bunk I sought to drown my sadness in a flood of tears. Idvor, with its sunny fields, vineyards, and orchards; with its grazing herds of cattle and flocks of sheep; with its beautiful church-spire

THE VILLAGE CHURCH IN IDVOR

and the solemn ringing of church-bells; with its merry boys and girls dancing to the tune of the Serbian bag-pipes the Kolo on the village green—Idvor, with all the familiar scenes that I had ever seen there, appeared before my tearful eyes, and in the midst of them I saw my mother listening to my sister reading slowly the letter which I had sent to her from Hamburg. Every one of these scenes seemed to start a new shower of tears, which finally cleared the oppressiveness of my spiritual atmosphere. I thought that I could hear my mother say to my sister: "God bless him for his affec-tionate letter. May the spirit of St. Sava guide him in the land beyond the seas! I know that he will make good his promises." Sadness deserted me then and I felt strong again.

He who has never crossed the stormy Atlantic dur-ing the month of March in the crowded steerage of an immigrant ship does not know what hardships are. I bless the stars that the immigration laws were different then than they are now, otherwise I should not be among the living. To stand the great hardships of a stormy sea when the rosy picture of the promised land is before your mind's eye is a severe test for any boy's nerve and physical stamina; but to face the same hard-ships as a deported and penniless immigrant with no cheering prospect in sight is too much for any person, unless that person is entirely devoid of every finer sensibility. Many a night I spent on the deck of that immigrant ship hugging the warm smoke-stack and adjusting my position so as to avoid the force of the gale and the sharpness of its icy chilliness. All I had was the light suit of clothes which I carried on my back. Everything else I had converted into money with which to cover my transportation expenses. There was nothing left to pay for a blanket and mattress for my steerage bunk. I could not rest there during the cold nights of March without much shivering and unbearable discomfort.

If it had not been for the warm smoke-stack I should have died of cold. At first I had to fight for my place there in the daytime, but when the immigrants understood that I had no warm clothing they did not disturb me any longer. I often thought of my yellow sheepskin coat and the black sheepskin cap, and understood more clearly than ever my mother's far-sightedness when she provided that coat and cap for my long journeys. A blast of the everlasting gales had carried away my hat, and a Turkish fez such as the Serbs of Bosnia wear was the only head-gear I had. It was providential that I had not succeeded in selling it in Prague. Most of my fellow emigrants thought that I was a Turk and cared little about my discomforts. But, nevertheless, I felt quite brave and strong in the daytime; at night, however, when, standing alone alongside of the smoke-stack, I beheld through the howling darkness the white rims of the mountain-high waves speeding on like maddened dragons toward the tumbling ship, my heart sank low. It was my implicit trust in God and in his regard for my mother's prayers which enabled me to overcome my fear and bravely face the horrors of the angry seas.

On the fourteenth day, early in the morning, the flat

coast-line of Long Island hove in sight. Nobody in the motley crowd of excited immigrants was more happy to see the promised land than I was. It was a clear, mild, and sunny March morning, and as we approached New York Harbor the warm sun-rays seemed to thaw out the chilliness which I had accumulated in my body by continuous exposure to the wintry blasts of the North Atlantic. I felt like a new person, and saw in every new scene presented by the New World as the ship moved into it a new promise that I should be welcome. Life and activity kept blossoming out all along the ship's course, and seemed to reach full bloom as we entered New York Harbor.

The scene which was then unfolded before my eyes was most novel and bewildering. The first impressions of Budapest and of Prague seemed like pale-faced images of the grand realities which New York Harbor disclosed before my eager eyes. A countless multitude of boats lined each shore of the vast river; all kinds of craft ploughed hurriedly in every direction through the waters of the bay; great masses of people crowded the numerous ferry-boats, and gave me the impression that one crowd was just about as anxious to reach one shore of the huge metropolis as the other was to reach the other shore; they all must have had some important thing to do, I thought.

The city on each side of the shore seemed to throb with activity. I did not distinguish between New York and Jersey City. Hundreds of other spots like the one I beheld, I thought, must be scattered over the vast territories of the United States, and in these seething pots of human action there must be some one activity,

I was certain, which needed me. This gave me courage. The talk which I had listened to during two weeks on the immigrant ship was rather discouraging, I thought. One immigrant was bragging about his long experience as a cabinetmaker, and informed his audience that cabinetmakers were in great demand in America; another one was telling long tales about his skill as a mechanician; a third one was spinning out long yarns about the fabulous agricultural successes of his relatives out West, who had invited him to come there and join them; a fourth confided to the gaping crowd that his brother, who was anxiously waiting for him, had a most prosperous bank in some rich mining-camp in Nevada where people never saw any money except silver and gold and hardly ever a coin smaller than a dollar; a fifth one, who had been in America before, told us in a rather top-lofty way that no matter who you were or what you knew or what you had you would be a greenhorn when you landed in the New World, and a greenhorn has to serve his apprenticeship before he can establish his claim to any recognition. He admitted, however, that immigrants with a previous practical training, or strong pull through relatives and friends, had a shorter apprenticeship. I had no practical training, and I had no relatives nor friends nor even acquaintances in the New World. I had nothing of any immediate value to offer to the land I was about to enter. That thought had discouraged me as I listened to the talks of the immigrants; but the activity which New York Harbor presented to my eager eyes on that sunny March day was most encouraging.

Presently the ship passed by Castle Garden, and I

heard some one say: "There is the Gate to America."
An hour or so later we all stood at the gate. The immigrant ship, *Westphalia*, landed at Hoboken and a
tug took us to Castle Garden. We were carefully ex-
amined and cross-examined, and when my turn came
the examining officials shook their heads and seemed
to find me wanting. I confessed that I had only five
cents in my pocket and had no relatives here, and that
I knew of nobody in this country except Franklin, Lincoln, and Harriet Beecher Stowe, whose "Uncle Tom's
Cabin" I had read in a translation. One of the officials,
who had one leg only, and walked with a crutch,
seemed much impressed by this remark, and looking
very kindly into my eyes and with a merry twinkle in
his eye he said in German: "You showed good taste
when you picked your American acquaintances." I
learned later that he was a Swiss who had served in
the Union army during the Civil War. I confessed also
to the examining officials that I had no training in the
arts and crafts, but that I was anxious to learn, and
that this desire had brought me to America.

In answer to the question why I had not stayed at
home or in Prague to learn instead of wandering across
the sea with so little on my back and nothing in my
pocket, I said that the Hungarian and Austrian authorities had formed a strong prejudice against me on
account of my sympathies with people, and particularly with my father, who objected to being cheated
out of their ancient rights and privileges which the
emperor had guaranteed to them for services which
they had been rendering to him loyally for nearly two
hundred years. I spoke with feeling, and I felt that I

made an impression upon the examiners, who did not look to me like officials such as I was accustomed to see in Austria-Hungary. They had no gold and silver braid and no superior airs but looked very much like ordinary civilian mortals.

That gave me courage and confidence, and I spoke frankly and fearlessly, believing firmly that I was addressing human beings who had a heart which was not held in bondage by cast-iron rules invented by their superiors in authority. The Swiss veteran who walked on crutches, having lost one of his legs in the Civil War, was particularly attentive while I was being cross-examined, and nodded approvingly whenever I scored a point with my answers. He whispered something to the other officials, and they finally informed me that I could pass on, and I was conducted promptly to the Labor Bureau of Castle Garden. My Swiss friend looked me up a little later and informed me that the examiners had made an exception in my favor and admitted me, and that I must look sharp and find a job as soon as possible.

As I sat in the Labor Bureau waiting for somebody to come along and pick me out as a worthy candidate for some job, I could not help surveying those of my fellow immigrants who, like myself, sat there waiting for a job. I really believed that they were in a class below me, and yet they had had no trouble in being admitted. They had not needed favors on the part of the officials in order to be admitted. I had, and therefore, I inferred, they must have appeared to the officials to be more desirable. It was true, I said, arguing

with myself, that they had a definite trade; they undoubtedly had some money; and they certainly looked
more prosperous than I did, judging by their clothes.
But why should the possession of a trade, of money, or
of clothes stand so much higher in America than it did
in Idvor, my native village? We had a blacksmith, a
wheelwright, and a barber in Idvor; they were our
craftsmen; and we had a Greek storekeeper who had a
lot of money and wore expensive city-made clothes,
but there was not one respectable Serb peasant in
Idvor, no matter how poor, who did not think that he
was superior to these people who had only a transient
existence in our historic village. The knowledge of our
traditions and our implicit belief in them made us feel
superior to people who wandered about like gypsies
with no traditions, and with nothing to anchor them
to a definite place. A newcomer to our village was
closely scrutinized, and he was judged not so much by
his skill in a craft, nor by his money, nor by his clothes,
but by his personality, by the reputation of his family,
and by the traditions of the people to whom he belonged.

The examiners at Castle Garden seemed to attach
no importance to these things, because they did not
ask me a single question concerning my family, the
history of my village, or the history of the military
frontier and of the Serb race. It was no wonder, said I,
consoling myself, that I appeared to them less desirable than many of the other immigrants who would
never have been allowed to settle in Idvor, and whose
society on the immigrant ship had interested me so little, and, in fact, had often been repulsive to me, be-

cause I could not help considering many of them a sort of spiritual muckers.

My admission by a special favor of the examiners was a puzzle and a disappointment to me, but it did not destroy the firmness of my belief that I brought to America something which the examiners were either unable or did not care to find out, but which, nevertheless, I valued very highly, and that was: a knowledge of and a profound respect and admiration for the best traditions of my race. My mother and the illiterate peasants at the neighborhood gatherings in Idvor had taught me that; no other lesson had ever made a deeper impression upon me.

## II

## THE HARDSHIPS OF A GREENHORN

My first night under the Stars and Stripes was spent in Castle Garden. It was a glorious night, I thought; no howling of the gales, no crashing of the waves, and no tumbling motion of the world beneath my feet, such as I had experienced on the immigrant ship. The feeling of being on *terra firma* sank deep into my consciousness and I slept the sound sleep of a healthy youth, although my bed was a bare floor. The very early morning saw me at my breakfast, enjoying a huge bowl of hot coffee and a big chunk of bread with some butter, supplied by the Castle Garden authorities at Uncle Sam's expense.

Then I started out, eager to catch a glimpse of great New York, feeling, in the words of the psalmist, "as a strong man ready to run a race." An old lady sat near the gate of Castle Garden offering cakes and candies for sale. A piece of prune pie caught my eye, and no true Serb can resist the allurements of prunes. It is a national sweetmeat. I bought it, paying five cents for it, the only money I had, and then I made a bee-line across Battery Park, at the same time attending to my pie. My first bargain in America proved a failure. The prune pie was a deception; it was a prune pie filled with prune pits, and I thought of the words of my fellow passenger on the immigrant ship who had said:

"No matter who you are or what you know or what you have you will be a greenhorn when you land in America." The prune-pie transaction whispered into my ear: "Michael, you are a greenhorn; this is the first experience in your life as a greenhorn. Cheer up! Get ready to serve your apprenticeship as a greenhorn before you can establish your claim to any recognition," repeating the words of my prophetic fellow passenger who had served his apprenticeship in America. No prophet ever uttered a truer word.

The old Stevens House, a white building with green window-shutters, stood at the corner of Broadway and Bowling Green. When I reached this spot and saw the busy beehive called Broadway, with thousands of telegraph-wires stretching across it like a cobweb between huge buildings, I was overawed, and wondered what it meant. Neither Budapest, nor Prague, nor Hamburg had looked anything like it. My puzzled and panicky expression and the red fez on my head must have attracted considerable attention, because suddenly I saw myself surrounded by a small crowd of boys of all sizes, jeering and laughing and pointing at my fez. They were newsboys and bootblacks, who appeared to be anxious to have some fun at my expense. I was embarrassed and much provoked, but controlled my Serbian temper.

Presently one of the bigger fellows walked up to me and knocked the fez off my head. I punched him on the nose and then we clinched. My wrestling experiences on the pasturelands of Idvor came to my rescue. The bully was down in a jiffy, and his chums gave a loud cheer of ringing laughter. I thought it was a signal for general attack, but they did not touch me nor interfere in any way. They acted like impartial spectators, anxious to see that the best man won. Suddenly I felt a powerful hand pulling me up by the collar, and when I looked up I saw a big official with a club in his hand and a fierce expression in his eye. He looked decidedly unfriendly, but after listening to the appeals of the newsboys and bootblacks who witnessed the fight he softened and handed me my fez. The boys who a little while before had jeered and tried to guy me evidently appealed in my behalf when the policeman interfered. They had actually become my friends. When I walked away toward Castle Garden, with my red fez proudly cocked up on my head, the boys cheered. I thought to myself that the unpleasant incident was worth my while, because it taught me that I was in a country where even among the street urchins there was a strong sentiment in favor of fair play even to a Serbian greenhorn. America was different from Austria-Hungary. I never forgot the lesson and never had a single reason to change my opinion.

A gentleman who had witnessed the fight joined me on my return trip to Castle Garden, and when we reached the employment bureau he offered me a job. When I learned that one of my daily duties would be to milk a cow, I refused. According to Serb traditions, milking a cow is decidedly a feminine job. Another gentleman, a Swiss foreman on a Delaware farm, offered me another job, which was to drive a team of mules and help in the work of hauling things to the field preparatory for spring planting. I accepted gladly, feeling confident that I knew all about driving animals, although I had never even seen a mule in all my experiences in Idvor. We left for Philadelphia that forenoon and caught there the early afternoon boat for Delaware City, where we arrived late in the afternoon.

As we passed through Philadelphia I asked the Swiss foreman whether that was the place where a hundred years before famous Benjamin Franklin flew his kite, and he answered that he had never heard of the gentleman, and that I must have meant William Penn. "No," said I, "because I never heard of this gentleman." "You have still to learn a thing or two about American history," said the Swiss foreman, with a superior air. "Yes, indeed," I said, "and I intend to do it as soon as I have learned a thing or two about the English language"; and I wondered whether the Swiss foreman who had never heard of Benjamin Franklin and his kite had really learned a thing or two in American history, although he had lived some fifteen years in the United States.

There were quite a number of farmers on the Delaware boat, every one of them wearing a long goatee but no mustache; such was the fashion at that time. Every one of them had the brim of his slouch hat turned down, covering his eyes completely. As they conversed they looked like wooden images; they made no gestures and I could not catch the expression of their hidden eyes; without these powerful aids to the understanding of the spoken word I could not make out a single syllable in their speech. The English language sounded to me like an inarticulate mode of speech, just as inarticulate as the joints of those imperturbable Delaware farmers. I wondered whether I should ever succeed in learning a thing or two in this most peculiar tongue. I thought of the peasants at the neighborhood gatherings in Idvor, and of their winged words, each of which found its way straight into my soul. There also appeared before my mental vision the image of Baba Batikin, with fire in his eye and a vibratory movement of his hand accompanying his stirring tales of Prince Marko. How different and how superior those peasants of Idvor appeared to me when I compared them with the farmers on that Delaware boat! "Impossible," said I, "that a Serb peasant should be so much superior to the American peasant!" Something wrong with my judgment, thought I, and I charged it to my being a greenhorn and unable to size up an American farmer.

At the boat-landing in Delaware City a farm-wagon was awaiting us, and we reached the farm at supper-time. The farm-buildings were fully a mile from the town, standing all by themselves; there was no village and there were no neighbors, and the place looked to me like a camp. There was no village life among American farmers, I was told, and I understood then why those farmers on the Delaware boat were so devoid of all animation. The farm-hands were all young fellows, but considerably older than myself, and when the foreman introduced me to them, by my Christian name, I found that most of them spoke German with a Swiss accent, the same which the foreman had who brought me from New York. One of them asked me how long I had been in the country, and when I told him that I was about twenty-four hours in the country, he smiled and said that he thought so, evidently on account of the unmistakable signs of a greenhorn which he saw all over me.

The first impression of an American farm was dismal. In the messroom, however, where supper was served, everything was neat and lovely, and the supper looked to me like a holiday feast. I became more reconciled to the American farm. The farm-hands ate much and spoke very little, and when they finished they left the dining-room without any ceremony. I was left alone, and moved my chair close to a warm stove and waited for somebody to tell me what to do next. Presently two women came in and proceeded to clear the supper-table; they spoke English and seemed to pay no attention to me. They probably thought that I was homesick and avoided disturbing me.

Presently I saw a young girl, somewhat younger than myself. She pretended to be helping the women, but I soon discovered that she had another mission. Her appearance reminded me of a young Vila, a Serbian fairy, who in the old Serbian ballads plays a most wonderful part. No hero ever perished through misfortune who had the good fortune to win the friendship of a Vila. Supernatural both in intelligence and in physical skill, the Vilæ could always find a way out of every difficulty. I felt certain that if there ever was a Vila this young girl was one. Her luminous blue eyes, her finely chiselled features, and her graceful movements made a strange impression upon me. I imagined that she could hear the faintest sound, that she could see in the darkest night, and that, like a real Vila, she could feel not only the faintest breezes but even the thoughts of people near her. She certainly felt my thoughts. Pointing to a table in a corner of the dining-room, she directed my attention to writing-paper and ink, placed there for the convenience of farm-hands. I understood her meaning, although I did not understand her words. I spent the evening writing a letter to my mother. This was my wish, and the Vila must have read it in my face.

One of the farm-hands, a Swiss, came in after a while in order to remind me that it was bedtime and to inform me that early in the morning he would wake me up and take me to the barn, where my job would be assigned to me. He kept his word, and with lantern in hand he took me long before sunrise to the barn and introduced me to two mules which he put in my charge. I cleaned them and fed them while he watched and directed; after breakfast he showed me how to harness and hitch them up. I took my turn in the line of teams hauling manure to the fields. He warned me not to apply myself too zealously to the work of loading and unloading, until I had become gradually broken in, otherwise I should be laid up stiff as a rod. The next day I was laid up, stiffer than a rod. He was much provoked, and called me the worst "greenhorn" that he ever saw. But, thanks to the skilled and tender care of the ladies on the farm, I was at my job again two days later. My being a greenhorn appealed to their sympathy; they seemed to have the same kind of soul which I had first observed in my American friends who paid my fare from Vienna to Prague.

One of my mules gave me much trouble, and the more he worried me the more amusement he seemed to furnish to the other farm-hands, rough immigrants of foreign birth. He did not bite, nor did he kick, as some of the mules did, but he protested violently against my putting the bridle on his head. The other farm-hands had no advice to offer; they seemed to enjoy my perplexity. I soon discovered that the troublesome mule could not stand anybody touching his ears. That was his ticklish spot. I finally got around it; I never took his bridle off on working-days, but only removed the bit, so that he could eat. On Sunday mornings, however, when I had all the time I wanted, I took his bridle off, cleaned it, and put it on, and did not remove it again for another week. The foreman and the superintendent discovered my trick and approved of it, and so the farm-hands lost the amusement which they had had at my expense every morning at the harnessing hour. I noticed that they were impressed by my trick and did not address me by the name of greenhorn quite so often. They were also surprised to hear me make successful attempts to speak English. Nothing counts so much in the immigrant's bid for promotion to a grade above that of a greenhorn as the knowledge of the English language. In these efforts I received a most unexpected assistance, and for that I was much indebted to my red fez.

On every trip from the barnyard to the fields, my mules and I passed by the superintendent's quarters, and there behind the wall of neatly piled-up cord-wood I observed every now and then the golden curls of my American Vila. She cautiously watched there, just like a Serbian Vila at the edge of a forest. My red fez perched up on a high seat behind the mules obviously attracted and amused her. Whenever I caught her eye I saluted in regular Balkan fashion, and it was a salute such as she had never seen before in the State of Delaware. Her curiosity seemed to grow from day to day, and so did mine.

One evening I sat alone near the warm stove in the messroom and she came in and said: "Good evening!" I answered by repeating her greeting, but pronounced it badly. She corrected me, and, when I repeated her greeting the second time, I did much better, and she applauded my genuine effort. Then she proceeded to teach me English words for everything in the dining-room, and before that first lesson was over I knew some twenty English words and pronounced them to her satisfaction. The next day I repeated these words aloud over and over again during my trips to the fields, until I thought that even the mules knew them by heart. At the second lesson on the following evening I scored a high mark from my teacher and added twenty more words to my English vocabulary. As time went on, my vocabulary increased at a rapid rate, and my young teacher was most enthusiastic. She called me "smart," and I never forgot the word. One evening she brought in her mother, who two weeks previously had taken care of me when I was laid up from overzealous loading. At that time she could not make me understand a single word she said. This time, however, I had no difficulty, and she was greatly surprised and pleased. My first examination in English was a complete success.

At the end of the first month on the Delaware farm my confidence in the use of the English language had grown strong. During the second month I grew bold enough to join in lengthy conversations. The superintendent's wife invited me often to spend the evening with the family. My tales of Idvor, Panchevo, Buda- pest, Prague, Hamburg, and the immigrant ship inter- ested them much, they said. My pronunciation and grammar amused them even more than they were will- ing to show. They were too polite to indulge in un- restrained laughter over my Serbian idioms. During these conversations the Vila sat still and seemed to be all attention. She was all eyes and ears, and I knew that she was making mental notes of every mistake in my grammar and pronunciation. At the next lesson she would correct every one of these mistakes, and then she watched at the next family gathering to see whether I should repeat them. But I did not; my highest ambition was to show myself worthy of the title "smart" which she had given me.

One evening I was relating to the superintendent's family how I had refused the first offer of a job at Castle Garden, because I did not care to accept the daily duty of milking a cow, which, according to my Serbian notions, was a purely feminine job. I admitted that Serbian and American notions were entirely dif- ferent in this particular respect, because, although over a hundred cows were milked daily on the farm, I never saw a woman in any one of the many barns, nor in the huge creamery. I confessed also that both the Vila and her mother would be entirely out of place not only in the cow-barns but even in the scrupulously clean creamery, adding that if the Vila had been obliged to attend to the cows and to the creamery, she would not have found the time to teach me English, and, there- fore, I preferred the American custom. Vila's mother was highly pleased with this remark and said: "Michael, my boy, you are beginning to understand our American ways, and the sooner you drop your Serbian notions the sooner you will become an American."

She explained to me the position of the American woman as that of the educator and spiritual guide of the coming generation, emphasizing the fact that the vast majority of teachers in American primary schools were women. This information astonished and pleased me, because I knew that my mother was a better teacher than my schoolmaster, an old man with a funny nasal twang. Her suggestion, however, that I should drop my Serbian notions and become an American as soon as possible disturbed me. But I said nothing; I was a greenhorn only and did not desire to express an opinion which might clash with hers. I thought it strange, however, that she took it for granted that I wished to become an American.

The next day was Sunday, and I walked to church, which was in Delaware City. The singing of hymns did not impress me much, and the sermon impressed me even less. Delaware City was much bigger than my native Idvor, and yet the religious service in Idvor was more elaborate. There was no choral singing in the church of Delaware City, and there were no ceremonies with a lot of burning candles and the sweet perfume of burning incense, and there was no ringing of harmonious church-bells. I was disappointed, and wondered why Vila's mother expected me to drop my Serbian notions and embrace America's ways, which, so far as public worship was concerned, appeared to me as less attractive than the Serbian ways. Vila's family met me in front of the church and asked me to ride home with them. A farm-hand riding in a fine carriage with his employer struck me as extraordinary, and I wished to be excused, but they insisted. No rich peasant in Idvor would have done that. In this respect Delaware farmers with their American ways appealed to me more.

Another surprise was in store for me: Vila's mother insisted that I share with the family their Sunday dinner, just as I had shared with them the divine service. I saw in it an effort on her part to show an appreciation of my religious habit and to encourage it, thus proving in practice what she preached to me about the spiritual influence of the American woman. During the dinner I described the Sundays of Idvor, dwelling particularly upon the custom among the Serbian boys and girls of kolo dancing on the village green in front of the church on Sunday afternoons. Vila approved of the custom enthusiastically, but her mother thought that a walk through the peach-orchards, which were then in full bloom, was at least as good. Vila and I walked together that Sunday afternoon. My attendance at church gained for me this favor also.

He who has never seen the Delaware peach-orchards of those days in full bloom, when in the month of May the ground is a deep velvety green, and when the Southern sky seen through the golden atmosphere of a sunny May day reminds one of those mysterious landscapes which form the background in some of Raphael's Madonna pictures—he who has never seen that glorious sight does not know the heavenly beauty of this little earth. No painter would dare attempt to put on canvas the cloth of flaming gold which on that balmy Sunday afternoon covered the ripples of the sun-kissed Delaware River. Vila asked me whether I had ever seen anything more beautiful in Idvor, and I said no, but added that nothing is as lovely and as sweet as one's native village. When I informed her that some day I expected to return to it, enriched by my experiences in America, she looked surprised and said:

"Then you do not intend to become an American?"

"No," said I; and after some hesitation I added: "I ran away from the military frontier because the rulers of the land wanted to transform me into a Hungarian; I ran away from Prague because I objected to Austrian Teutonism; I shall run away from Delaware City also if, as your good mother suggested, I am expected to drop my Serbian notions and become an American. My mother, my native village, my Serbian orthodox faith, and my Serbian language and the people who speak it are my Serbian notions, and one might as well expect me to give up the breath of my life as to give up my Serbian notions."

"You misunderstood my mother, Michael," said the Vila; "she only referred to your notions about woman's work, and you know that European women are expected to do the hard work for which only men are strong enough."

"Very true," said I; "the strongest and ablest men in Europe spend the best part of their lives on battle-fields, or training for the battle-fields; this is particularly true of the Serbian people. This forces our Serbian women to do some of the hard work which men should do." This gave me a fitting opportunity to say a few things in favor of the spiritual influence of the Serbian women by describing the position of the Serbian woman as she is represented in the Serbian ballads—of Chuchuk Stana, the wife of Hayduk Velyko, who urged her hero husband to sacrifice his life rather than surrender the eastern frontier of Serbia, which, during the Serbian revolution, he was defending against vastly superior Turkish forces; of the maid of Kossovo, who at the risk of her life and liberty visited the battle-field of Kossovo in order to administer the last spiritual aid to the fallen and dying heroes; of Yevrosima, mother of Prince Marko, the national hero of the Serbian race, whose counsel and advice were the only guiding star to Marko throughout his stormy life. I told her also that I should not be a witness to that heavenly scene on the banks of the Delaware that Sunday afternoon if it had not been for my mother, who had urged me to go into the world and learn new things, which I could not learn in my native peasant village.

Young Vila was much impressed by my Serbian tales, and by my pleading in behalf of the Serbian women, and then she asked me whether I had ever heard of Martha Washington, the wife of George Washington, the national hero of America. I confessed complete ignorance. Pointing to the golden ripples of the sun-kissed Delaware River, she said that it did not always look as bright and peaceful, and then described its appearance when in the middle of winter its surface is covered with broken ice, which, tossed by the waves of the angry river, makes a passage across it next to impossible. But in January, 1777, George Washington, the commander of the retreating American armies, crossed it, and on the other side of the river, near Trenton, surprised the advancing victorious British armies and defeated them, turning American defeat into American victory. "Washington," she said, "just like Hayduk Velyko, was ready to sacrifice his life while crossing the treacherous ice-fields of the angry Delaware in order to strike a timely blow for the safety of his country." And she was inclined to believe, she said, that Martha Washington acted at that critical moment just as Chuchuk Stana did. From that day on, Washington was to me the Hayduk Velyko of America, and the name of the Delaware River inspired me always with thoughts of deep veneration.

Vila showed me that America, like Serbia, was also a land of heroes. The rest of that glorious Sunday afternoon was spent in Vila's answering my numerous questions concerning George Washington and the war of the American Revolution. It was the most inspiring afternoon which I had experienced in America, and I felt that, after all, there might be many things in America which were just as great as those great things of which the Serbian guslar sings in the national ballads of Serbia. Vila had succeeded in welding the first link between my Serbian traditions and the traditions of America. I apologized to her for misunderstanding her mother's suggestion that I become an American as soon as possible, and confessed that I was much less anxious than I had thought I was a few moments before to run away from the shores of the historic Delaware.

After Vila discovered my lively interest in American history, she continued her English lessons to me by telling me stories relating to early American history, which I repeated to her. Jamestown, South St. Mary, in southern Maryland, and Virginia figured big in these tales. When I first heard of the *Mayflower,* a year or so later, and of its landing at Plymouth Rock, I wondered why Vila never mentioned that great historical event. She never mentioned Lincoln, and changed conversation when I once called him the American Prince Marko. America north of the Delaware River was very little in her mind, and even Philadelphia was mentioned only on account of the Liberty Bell and the Declaration of Independence.

One evening, Vila's mother asked me about my mother and her hopes for my future. Remembering her remarks concerning the spiritual influence of the American women upon the coming generation, I gave her a glowing account of my mother, and wound up by saying that she did not expect me to become an American farmer, and that I came to America to learn what I could not learn in a peasant country like that of my native village. She was much touched, and then in simple and solemn language she revealed to me a new truth which I never forgot and which I found confirmed by all my experiences in this great land, the truth, namely, that this is a country of opportunities which are open equally to all; that each individual must seek these opportunities and must be prepared to make good use of them when he finds them. She commended me warmly for making good use of all the opportunities which I had found on the farm, and advised me strongly to go in search of new opportunities.

Vila agreed with her, and I prepared to leave the hospitable shores of Delaware.

I made my return trip to Philadelphia on the same boat which had brought me to Delaware City. Things looked different from what they had on my first trip. The farmers of Delaware, my fellow passengers on the boat, did not look like wooden images, and their speech was not inarticulate. I understood their language, and its meaning found a sympathetic response in me. The trip reminded me much of the trip on the Danube some eighteen months prior to that time. One of my fellow passengers, a youngster of about my age, pointed out a place to me which he called Trenton, and assured me that the boat was passing over the spot where Washington crossed the Delaware. His geography was faulty as I found out much later. But it was swallowed by a greenhorn like me and it thrilled me, and I remembered then the first view of the Cathedral of Karlovci, the seat of the Serbian Patriarch, which was pointed out to me from the Danube boat by the theological students. I felt the same thrill in each case, and I knew that America was getting a hold upon my Serbian heart-strings. My appearance attracted no attention, either on the boat or at Philadelphia after we landed. My hat and clothes were American, but my heavy top-boots, so useful on the farm, were somewhat too heavy for the warm June days in Philadelphia.

The Swiss foreman had directed me to a Swiss acquaintance of his who had a small hotel in Philadelphia. He was very eager to have me take all my meals at the hotel, but my total capital of ten dollars made me cautious; besides, my days from early morning till late at night were spent in the heart of the city. No other human being ever saw so much of Philadelphia during a stay of five days as I did, hunting for a job, searching new opportunities, as Vila's mother expressed it. But I searched in vain. I gained new information about William Penn and Benjamin Franklin and saw many buildings the history of which is attached to these two great names, and I wondered why Benjamin Franklin ever deserted Boston to search new opportunities in a place like Philadelphia. But he did it, and succeeded. I was sure that neither he nor any other human being could walk more or chase after a job more diligently than I did, but then he was an American boy and he had a trade, and I was a Serbian greenhorn who did not know anything in particular, except how to drive a pair of mules. Besides, thought I, Philadelphia might have lost its wealth of opportunities since Franklin's days.

Such was my consolation while resting on a bench in Fairmount Park, near the grounds which were being prepared for the Centennial Exposition of 1876. I was lunching on a chunk of bread and thinking what would happen when the last three dollars, the remnant of my ten dollars which I brought from the Delaware farm, disappeared. A husky farmer approached me and addressed me in English, asking whether I wanted a job. "I do," said I; "I have been chasing after one nearly a week, and I can't chase much longer, because I see that my weary farm-boots are showing many signs of distress in their long daily struggles against these hot Philadelphia pavements."

A day later found me in South St. Mary, in southern Maryland. I expected great things here, having heard so much of its early history from Vila. I was engaged to drive a pair of mules, dragging cultivators through corn and tobacco fields. As far as skill and physical exertion were concerned, the job was easy. But the climate was deadly, and social life was even more so. The only interesting people whom I found there were those buried in the old cemetery, some two hundred years prior to that time, when South St. Mary was quite an important place, and when the original settlers brought many fine things from England, and even bricks with which they built their houses.

The only diversion I found was to read the legends on the tombstones in the old cemetery near the village church. Chesapeake Bay and the Potomac River and the many inlets of the bay bordered by luxuriant vegetation gave the country a most picturesque appearance. The flourishing corn and tobacco fields suggested prosperity, but the only people who stirred and showed any activity were darkies, whose language I could not understand. I felt that as far as human speech was concerned, I was in a valley of silence, although the air was full of incessant sounds from all kinds of insects and water-animals. Mosquitoes, gnats, and flies, and the most oppressive, almost tropical, heat of the sun made work in the fields unbearable. Many a time while driving the phlegmatic mules through the broiling atmosphere of the tobacco-fields I thought of the icy blasts of the North Atlantic which I had experienced on the immigrant ship less than three months before, and I prayed that one of those icy breaths of the polar regions might wander astray and reach the flatlands of Chesapeake Bay. My prayer was not heard, and I was happy to be still alive at the end of the month, and then I took my wages of fifteen dollars and made a bee-line for the north. I hoped that in New York I might be able to catch some of the cold North Atlantic breezes, and, after cooling off, pick up one of the many opportunities in the metropolis, which on the day when the immigrant ship landed me at Hoboken seemed to be seething with life and activity and brimful of all kinds of opportunities.

The Chesapeake boat landed me at Baltimore in the early hours of a Sunday morning, and the sound of beautifully tuned church-bells greeted me. I was told that Baltimore was a Catholic city and that the bells belonged to a Catholic cathedral. They almost persuaded me to stay in Baltimore and become a Roman Catholic, so sweet and soothing was their effect upon my soul. It recalled to my memory the lovely harmony of the church-bells of my native Idvor, and with that memory there appeared in my imagination the vision of my strongly orthodox mother and of St. Sava. This vision reminded me that I must say good-by to Roman Catholic Baltimore.

Forty-two years later I met Cardinal Gibbons in Baltimore during a visit to that city, when Johns Hopkins University conferred upon me the honorary LL.D. degree. I told him of the incident just referred to; he was in a jocular mood and said: "Too bad that you did not yield to the first effect of the Baltimore church-bells; you might be to-day the archbishop of this diocese, and perhaps even a cardinal." "But, in that case,

I should not have to-day the honorary LL.D. degree of Johns Hopkins; I would not exchange that for any other honor," said I, returning jest for jest and watching the merry twinkle in the cardinal's fluorescent eyes.

Some months later President Butler, of Columbia University, and I happened to be descending in the same lift at the Shoreham Hotel in Washington. Presently Cardinal Gibbons entered, and President Butler introduced me to his Eminence, who, recalling our former meeting in Baltimore, said, "I know Professor Pupin, and it is a great honor, indeed, to ride in the same lift with two eminent men who carry so many distinguished academic honors," and, as he looked at me with a genial smile which was brimful of Irish humor, I knew that he wished to remind me in a good-natured way of my high rating of an honorary Johns Hopkins degree in comparison with the honors attached to the titles of archbishop and cardinal.

The Pennsylvania train from Baltimore to New York delivered me to a ferry-boat, which landed me on West Street, where I found a small hotel kept by a German, a native of Friesland. He was a rugged old fellow who loved his low-German dialect, which I did not understand. He spoke in English to me, which, according to his son Christian, was much worse than mine, although he had been in America some twenty years. Christian was a yellow-haired and freckle-faced lad, of about my age, and we hit it off very well, forming a cross-matched team. He would have given anything, he said, to have my black hair and dark-red complexion. His almost white eyebrows and eyelashes and mischievous gray eyes and yellow freckles fascinated me. He was born in Hoboken and understood his father's low-German dialect, but whenever addressed in it, by his father or by the Friesland sailors who frequented his father's inn, he always answered in English, or, as he called it, "United States."

Christian managed somehow to get away every now and then from the little hotel and to accompany me on my many long errands in search of a job. His familiarity with the town helped me much to master the geography of New York, and to find out what's what and who's who in the great metropolis. He seemed to be the only opportunity which New York offered to me, and it was a great one. Every other opportunity which appeared in newspaper advertisements had hundreds of applicants, and they were lined up at the place of the promised opportunity, no matter how early Christian and I reached the place. I was quite sure that those opportunity-chasers lined up soon after the first issue of the morning papers. I was told that the year before (in 1873) occurred the Black Friday panic, and that New York had not yet recovered from it. There were thousands of unemployed, although it was summer.

One morning Christian told me that he had found a fine job for me, and he took me to a tug anchored quite near his father's hotel. There were quite a number of husky laborers on the tug, which took us to the German docks in Hoboken. We were to stay there and help in the loading of ships, replacing the longshoremen who were on strike. The job assigned to me was to assist the sailors who were painting the ship and things on the ship. We never left the docks until the strike was over, which lasted about three weeks. At its termination I was paid and the tug delivered me to the little hotel on West Street, where Christian received me with open arms. I had thirty dollars in my pocket, and Christian told me that I looked as rich as Commodore Vanderbilt, whom Christian considered to be the richest man in New York. Christian took me to Chatham Square to buy a new suit of clothes and other wearing apparel, and I thought that the Jewish clothing dealers would cause a riot fighting for my patronage.

The next day when I appeared at the breakfast-table in my new togs, Christian's father could hardly recognize me, but when he did he slapped me on the back and exclaimed: "Who would ever think that you are a Serbian greenhorn?" "Nobody," said Christian, resenting his father's remark, and then he added with some hesitation: "But who would ever think that you are not a German greenhorn?" Christian's father rebuked him and assured me that he meant no offense when he jokingly called me a Serbian greenhorn.

Christian was anxious to have me replenish my fortune, which was considerably reduced by my purchases in Chatham Square. He called my attention that morning to a big German who was drinking beer at the hotel bar after delivering several baskets filled with bread, rolls, and pies, and said that he was a rich and stingy baker, whose wagon, standing in front of the hotel, needed painting badly. I saw that the lettering needed speedy restoration. I assured my chum that my experience as assistant to the sailor painters on the Hoboken docks, in addition to my natural skill in free-hand drawing, qualified me for the job of restoring the lettering; Christian chuckled and made a bee-line for the stingy German baker. I got the contract to restore the lettering for five dollars and my meals, he to pay for the paints and the brushes, which were to remain my property. Christian formulated the contract and specified its terms very clearly; he was my business manager, and he enjoyed it hugely.

The next day I lunched with the baker's family, according to the terms of the contract, and after luncheon, as soon as the wagon had returned from its daily route, I started the work, interrupted by the supper only, and at nine o'clock in the evening the job was finished to the full satisfaction of the party of the first part. That evening found me richer by five dollars, several paint pots and brushes, a huge home-made apple pie, and a new and encouraging experience. Christian, for some reason unknown to me at that time, seemed to look upon the whole affair as a joke, but nevertheless he paid many compliments to my success as an artist. The next day we left bright and early for his father's house in Hoboken, where in accordance with a plan conceived by Christian we were to spend some time in painting and papering several of the rooms.

Profiting by the instructions which we received in sundry places, and after making several unsuccessful attempts, we managed to master the art and to finish the rooms to the full satisfaction of Christian's father, who confessed that no Hoboken expert could have done better. "This painting is much better than that which you did on the baker's wagon," he said, "because you added some dryer to the paint." "Right you are," said Christian, "but I am to blame, because I purposely avoided telling Michael to use some dryer on the baker's wagon. I wanted to make two jobs out of one." "There will be several jobs, I am afraid," said Christian's father, "because on the day after the lettering was done the baker's wagon was caught in a shower and all the fresh paint has been washed off, and the wagon looks like a show." Christian roared with laughter, but seeing that I looked worried he whispered in my ear: "Don't worry, it serves him right; he wanted a twenty-dollar job done for five dollars, because he took you for a greenhorn." Christian made a new arrangement for the relettering of the wagon and I earned another five dollars, but no home-made apple pie. The German baker in Goerck Street was neither as cordial nor as hospitable as he was before.

Christian encouraged me in the belief that I was a painter and paper-hanger, and I felt that I had a trade; that feeling gave me much confidence. Christian's mental attitude was a revelation to me. He actually believed that a boy can learn anything quickly and well enough to earn a living, if he will only try. He certainly could do anything, I thought, as I watched him in his little carpenter-shop in Hoboken. He also had a lathe and was quite expert in wood and metal turning, although he never served apprenticeship, as they do in Europe, in order to learn these things. When I told Christian that, according to my information on the immigrant ship, I was doomed to serve in America my apprenticeship as a greenhorn, he said that a European greenhorn must have told me that, and added, in an offhand manner, that I would be a greenhorn as long only as I thought that I was one.

My description of a European apprenticeship amused him much, and he called it worse than the slavery which was abolished here by the Civil War only a few years prior to that date. When I asked him where he got all those strange notions, he told me that these notions were not strange but genuine American notions, and that he first got them from his mother, who was a native American. His father and his father's German friends, he admitted, had the same notions as that greenhorn on the immigrant ship. Christian certainly looked like a Friesland German, but his thoughts, his words, and his manner of doing things were entirely different from anything I ever saw in Europe. He was my first glimpse of an American boy, just as the Vila on the Delaware farm was my first vision of an American girl, and her mother my first ideal of a noble American woman. They were the first to raise that mysterious curtain which prevents the foreign-born from seeing the soul of America, and when I caught a glimpse of it I loved it. It reminded me of the soul of my good people in Idvor, and I felt much more at home. The idea of being a greenhorn lost many of its horrifying features.

Christian left New York during that autumn to go into a shop in Cleveland. Without him, West Street had no attractions for me. I moved to the East Side of New York, so as to be near Cooper Union and its hospitable library. I spent many hours in it after my days of labor, or after my numerous unsuccessful daily trips in search of employment. It was my spiritual refuge when things looked black and hopeless. As winter approached, jobs grew alarmingly scarce, and my money was rapidly approaching the zero level. My hall-room in Norfolk Street was cheerless and cold, worse even than my little attic in Prague. Neither the room nor its neighborhood attracted me in daytime; I preferred to walk along the endless avenues. This exercise kept me warm and gave me a chance to make frequent inquiries for a job at painters' and paper-hangers' shops.

When the prospects for work of this kind appeared hopeless, I struck a new idea. Instead of walking more or less aimlessly, in order to keep myself warm and familiarize myself with the ways of the great city, I followed coal-carts, and when they dropped the coal on the sidewalk I rang the bell and offered my services to transfer the coal from sidewalk to cellar. I often got the job, which sometimes was a stepping-stone to other less humble and more remunerative employment. After placing the coal in the cellar and getting my pay, I would often suggest to the owner that his cellar and basement needed painting badly; most cellars and basements do. The owner on being informed that I was a painter out of work, a victim of the economic crisis, often yielded. The idea of a young and ambitious painter being compelled to carry coal from sidewalk to cellar at fifty cents a ton made a strong plea, stronger than any eloquence could make. The scheme worked well; it did not lead to affluence, but my room-rent was always paid on time, and I never starved. Often and often, however, I had to keep my appetite in check. I always had enough to buy my bowl of hot coffee and a brace of crullers for breakfast in a restaurant on wheels, stationed near Cooper Union, where Third Avenue car-drivers took their coffee on cold winter mornings.

During periods of financial stringency my lunches were a bowl of bean soup and a chunk of brown bread, which the Bowery Mission supplied for five cents. It was a splendid meal on those cold winter days. But the Bowery Mission supplied a prayer-meeting with red-hot speeches as dessert; some of these addresses I really enjoyed; there were speakers, however, who offended me, because they confessed that they were reformed drunkards and godless men, and they assured their hearers, victims of the economic crisis just like myself, that they would prosper if they would only sign the pledge and vow to return to Jesus. I neither drank nor had I ever deserted Jesus; the reformed drunkard's views of human life depressed me and drove me away from the Bowery Mission and from the Bowery.

Carrying coal from sidewalks to cellars and shovelling snow from sidewalks during that memorable winter were healthful jobs and cheerful enough, but not very remunerative; painting cellars and basements on Lexington Avenue was more remunerative, but fearfully depressing. To spend one's time day after day in dark cellars and basements and pass the night in a cheerless hall-room in Norfolk Street, surrounded by neighbors who were mostly foreign-born of the most unattractive type, was too much for a Serbian youth who knew the beautiful world as one sees it from the pasture-lands of his native village and from the banks of golden Delaware. The reading-room of the Cooper Union library relieved somewhat my mental depression, although it was packed with sad-looking victims of the economic crisis, who found their way from the Bowery to the reading-room in order to keep warm. I longed to see God's world of the country again.

The opportunity came, and about the middle of April of that year, 1875, I was on a farm in Dayton, New Jersey. My employer's family consisted of his wife and an elderly daughter, and I was the only farmhand on the place. They were apparently pleased with my work, and the ladies took much interest in my personal welfare. But the farmer, call him Mr. Brown, took it into his head that a youth who had lived one whole winter in Norfolk Street, New York, near the ungodly Bowery, needed spiritual regeneration. He was a very pious Baptist, and I soon discovered that in his everlasting professions of omissions and commissions he was even worse than that reformed drunkard whose sermons had driven me away from the Bowery Mission and its vigorous bean soup.

Every Sunday his family took me to church twice and made me sit between the female members of the family. I felt that the congregation imagined that Mr. Brown and his family were trying their best to convert a godless foreign youth and make a good Baptist out of him. Mr. Brown seemed to be in a great hurry about it, because every evening he made me listen for an hour at least to his reading of the Bible, and before we parted for the night he would offer a loud and fervent prayer that the Lord might kindle his light in the souls of those who had been wandering in darkness. I know

now that he had in mind the words of St. Luke, "To give
light to them that sit in darkness," but at that time I
fancied that he referred to my painting operations in
the cellars and basements of Lexington Avenue, and
interpreted his prayers as having a special reference
to me.

The joy of life which during the day I inhaled in the
fresh fields of the early spring was smothered in the
evening by Mr. Brown's views of religion, which were
views of a decrepit old man who thought of heaven
only because he had no terrestrial problems to solve.
He did his best to strip religion of every vestige of its
poetic beauty, and of its soul-stirring spiritual force,
and to make it appear like a mummy of a long-depart-
ed Egyptian corpse. A Serbian youth who looks to St.
Sava, the educator, and to the Serbian national ballads for an interpretation of the Holy Scriptures, could
not be expected to warm up for the religion which
farmer Brown preached. I thought of Vila and her
mother on the banks of the golden Delaware, and of
the glorious opportunities which they pointed out
ahead of me, and I wondered whether farmer Brown
was one of these opportunities; if so, then there were
some opportunities in America from which I wished to
run away.

One Sunday evening, after the church service, farmer
Brown introduced me to some of his friends, informing
them that I was a Serbian youth who had not enjoyed
all the opportunities of American religious training,
but that I was making wonderful progress, and that
some day I might even become an active member of
their congregation. The vision of my orthodox moth-

NASSAU HALL, PRINCETON UNIVERSITY

er, of the little church in Idvor, of the Patriarch in Karlovci, and of St. Sava, shot before my eyes like a flash, and I vowed to furnish a speedy proof that farmer Brown was wrong.

The next day I was up long before sunrise, having spent a restless night formulating a definite plan of deliverance from the intolerable boredom inflicted upon me by a hopeless religious crank. The eastern sky was like a veil of gold and it promised the arrival of a glorious April day. The fields, the birds, the distant woods, and the friendly country road all seemed to join in a melodious hymn of praise to the beauties of the wanderer's freedom. I bade good-by to the hospitable home of farmer Brown and made a bee-line for the distant woods. There the merry birds, the awakening buds on the blushing twigs, and the little wild flowers of the early spring seemed to long for the appearance of the glorious sun in the eastern sky. I did not, because I was anxious to put as much distance as possible between farmer Brown and myself before he knew that I had departed. When the sun was high in the heavens I made a halt and rested at the edge of woods on the side of a hill. A meadow was at my feet, and I, recalling the words of poet Nyegosh, watched for "the bright-eyed dewdrops to glide along the sunbeams to the heavens above." The distant view as seen from the elevation of my resting-place disclosed, near the horizon, the silhouette of a town with towers and high roofs looking like roofs of churches.

After some three additional hours of wandering, I crossed a bridge over a canal and found the distant town. There seemed to be one street only where busi-

saw the academic halls of Princeton gradually disappear in the distance and realized at the same time that the train was taking me back to the Bowery. Eight years later I read the letter which I wrote to my mother describing Princeton, in which, in order to encourage her, I had expressed a strong hope that some day I might write to her and sign myself a student at Princeton.

I may add here that my good friend Henry Fairfield Osborn, the distinguished scientist, was a sophomore at Princeton during that year. He might have looked just like that gentle youth who showed me the way to the railroad-station. President Wilson entered Princeton in the autumn of that year.

# III

## THE END OF THE APPRENTICESHIP AS GREENHORN

THE visions of Princeton persisted in my mind like after effects of strong light upon the retina. That gentle youth's suggestion that he might some day see me enrolled as a student at Princeton kept ringing in my ears, and sounded like mockery. A peasant boy from a Serb village who a little over two years previously was wearing a peasant's sheepskin coat and cap to become a fellow student of those youths who looked like young aristocrats seemed impossible. A European aristocrat would never have suggested such a thing, and that puzzled me. I saw an endless chain of difficult things between me and my enrolment as a student at Princeton, the home for gentle American youth. Social unpreparedness, I felt, was a much more serious difficulty than unpreparedness in things which one can learn from books. This difficulty could not be overcome by associating with people east of the Bowery, and I was heading that way. The nearer the train approached New York the less anxious I was to return to it. From Nassau Hall to the Bowery was too abrupt a change, and from the Bowery to Nassau Hall the change would have been even more abrupt. I compromised and looked up Christian's home on West Street.

Christian was still in Cleveland, but his father received me with open arms and promised to find me a job. In less than a week he found me one in a famous cracker factory on Cortlandt Street. An acquaintance of his with the name Eilers, a Frieslander and distant relative of a famous German writer of that name, was employed there; he steered me during my first experiences in the factory. A place was given me in a squad of boys and girls who punched the firm's name upon a particular kind of biscuit. The job was easy from the point of view of physical strength, but it required much manual dexterity. In spite of my ambition to advance to a high place in the squad I progressed very slowly.

I soon discovered that in manual dexterity the American boys and girls stood very high; my hands moved fairly rapidly after some practice, but theirs vibrated. I made up my mind that America was not a field in which I should gather many laurels by efforts requiring much manual dexterity. That idea had occurred to me before, when I first observed Christian handling his lathe. One day I was at the delivery desk of the Cooper Union Library, showing my library check to a youth behind the desk who countersigned it before a book was delivered to me. I noticed that he wrote rapidly, using sometimes his right hand and sometimes his left with equal ease and with much skill. "How can I ever compete with American boys," said I, "when they can write with either hand better than I can write with my right hand!"

There never was a doubt in my mind that American adaptability which I observed on every occasion was in a great measure due to manual training which young people used to get here. Christian's suggestion, mentioned above, that "a boy can learn anything quickly and well enough to earn a living if he will only try," I saw in a new light, when I watched the work of those boys and girls in the factory. Yes, American boys can, but not European, thought I. Lack of early manual training was a handicap which I felt on every step during my early progress in America. My whole experience confirmed me in the belief that manual training of the youth gives them a discipline which schoolbooks alone can never give. I discovered later that three of the greatest characters in American history, Franklin, Jefferson, and Lincoln, excelled in practical arts requiring dexterity, and that the constructive genius of the American nation can, in part, be traced to the discipline which one gets from early manual training.

The great opportunities which, according to my good friends on the Delaware farm, awaited me in this country were certainly not in the direction of arts requiring great manual dexterity. The country of baseball offered, I thought, very few opportunities in this direction to a foreign-born boy. I was convinced of that every time I made a comparison between myself and the other boys who were doing the same manual work in the factory that I did. They were my superiors. In one thing, however, I thought I was their superior. They did not know much about the latest things described in the *Scientific American,* nor in the scientific supplements of the Sunday *Sun,* which I read assiduously with the aid of a pocket dictionary.

The educational opportunities in the factory also escaped them. Jim, the boiler-room engineer and fireman of the factory, became interested in my scientific reading and encouraged me by paying several compliments to my interest in these things. He once suggested that some day, perhaps, I might become his scientific assistant in the boiler-room, if I did not mind shovelling coal and attending to the busy fires. He was joking, but I took him seriously. Every morning before the factory started I was with Jim, who was getting the steam up and preparing to blow the whistle and start the wheels going. I volunteered to assist him "shovelling coal and attending to the busy fires," and after a time I understood the manipulations in the boiler-room quite well, according to Jim. The steam-engine excited my liveliest interest. It was the first opportunity that I had ever had to study at close range the operations of a steam-engine, and I made the most of it, thanks to Jim's patient interest in my thirst for new information. He was my first professor in engineering.

One exceptionally hot afternoon during that summer found Jim prostrated by heat and I volunteered to run the boiler-room until he got well. I did it during the rest of that afternoon, much to the surprise of everybody, but was not allowed to continue, because a fireman's license was required for that. When Jim returned I urged him to help me get a license, but he answered that an intelligent boy, eager to learn, should not cross the Atlantic for the purpose of becoming a fireman. "You must aim higher, my lad," said Jim, and he added that if I continued to make good use of my pocket dictionary and of my scientific reading I should soon outgrow the opportunities offered by the New England Cracker Factory in Cortlandt Street. He never missed a chance to encourage me and to promise new successes for new efforts. In that respect he reminded me much of my mother.

Jim was a humble fireman and boiler-room engineer; his early education was scanty, so that he was not much on books; but he stood in awe in the presence of books. Referring to my habit of carrying a pocket dictionary in my hip pocket and looking up in it the meaning and the pronunciation of every word which was new to me, he would exclaim, jokingly, "Look in the book," whenever some obscure points arose in our boiler-room discussions. His admiration for books was much increased when I related to him the story of James Watt and his experiments with the steam-engine, a story which I had dug out in an old encyclopædia in the Cooper Union Library. When I told him that James Watt had perfected his steam-engine and thus started the development of the modern steam-engine several years before the Declaration of Independence, he dropped a remark which I never forgot. He said: "The English made us write the Declaration of Independence, and they also gave us the steam-engine with which we made our independence good." Jim was not much on learning but he was brimful of native practical philosophy.

Jim had a relative attending classes at Cooper Union and encouraged me to join several of its evening classes, which I did. I reported to him regularly the new things which I learned there. This practice benefited me even

Some of these men were: Morse, the first promoter of the electric telegraph; Joseph Henry, the great physicist, head of the Smithsonian Institution, and founder of scientific bureaus in Washington; McCormick, the inventor of the reaper; Howe, the inventor of the sewing-machine; Ericsson, the engineer of the *Monitor,* and so forth. My study of their lives was a timely preparation for my visit to Philadelphia, to see the Centennial Exposition, the preparatory work for which I had seen two years prior to that time, when, returning from the Delaware farm, I stopped at Philadelphia to search for opportunities.

The work of those great captains of industry forming the group in the great painting, "Men of Progress," was in evidence in every nook and corner of the Centennial Exposition. This great show impressed me as a splendid glorification of all kinds of wonderful mechanisms, driven by steam and animal power, which helped to develop the great resources of the United States. All scientific efforts exhibited there concerned themselves with the question of what things can do, rather than what they are. The show was also a glorification of the great men who first formulated, clearly stated, and fought for the ideals of the United States. I saw that fact proclaimed in many of the historical features of the exposition, and I did not fail to understand clearly that the show took place in Philadelphia because the Liberty Bell and the Declaration of Independence were first heard in Philadelphia. When I left Philadelphia and its show I carried away in my head a good bit of American history. The Americanization process which was going on within me was very much

*From an engraving by John Sartain after a painting by J. Schussele, reproduced by the courtesy of Cooper Union*

Dr. Morton  Colt  Saxton  Peter Cooper  Professor Henry Ericsson  Bigelow
Bogardus  Goodyear  Dr. Mott  Burden  Jennings
McCormick  Mott  Sickles  Morse  Hoe  Blanchard  Howe

MEN OF PROGRESS—AMERICAN INVENTORS

speeded up by what I saw at the Centennial Exposition.

On my return to New York I told Jim, the fireman, that he was right when he said: "The English made us write the Declaration of Independence, and they also gave us the steam-engine with which we made our independence good." But, instructed by my study of the lives of men who were represented in the painting "Men of Progress," and by what I learned at the Philadelphia exposition of these men and of the leaders of the American Revolution, I suggested to Jim that the steam-engine without great men behind it would have been of little avail. "Yes," said Jim, "the Declaration of Independence without men of character and brains behind it would also have been of little avail; and the great aims of the Civil War without men like Lincoln and Grant behind them would have ended in a foolish fizzle. This country, my lad," exclaimed Jim with much warmth, "is a monument to the lives of the men of brains and character and action who made it."

Jim threw out this chunk of wisdom with the same ease and in the same offhand manner which he displayed when he threw a few shovelfuls of coal upon the busy fires under his boilers. To him it was an obvious truth; to a lad like myself, who was accustomed to look upon countries as monuments to kings and princes and their victorious armies, it was a revelation; and I said so. This brought from Jim another epigrammatic remark to the effect that my trip to America would teach me nothing if it did not teach me first to squeeze out of my mind all foolish European notions and make room for new ideas which I might pick up here and there in this new world. Jim's sayings were always short and to the point and their record in my mind never faded.

Jim was very popular with everybody in the factory, and the fact that he thought well of me improved my standing much. A Mr. Paul, the youngest and most active member of the New England Cracker Factory in Cortlandt Street, paid frequent visits to the boiler-room. I had an idea that Jim's views of things interested him just as much as the operations of the boiler-room. One morning he made a very early visit before the steam-whistle had blown and the steam-engine had started on its daily routine, and he found me in the boiler-room, a busy volunteer fireman. Jim introduced me to him in a jocular way as a student who found his way from Princeton to Cortlandt Street, where in daytime I was rapidly learning every trick of the biscuit industry while in the evening I was absorbing all the wisdom of Cooper Union.

A few days later Mr. Paul informed me that my fame as a painter of baker-wagons and of basements on Lexington Avenue, and also my record as a student in mechanical drawing in the evening classes of Cooper Union, had reached the board of directors of the New England Cracker Factory, and that they had resolved to offer me a new job. I was advanced to the position of assistant to the shipping clerk. It meant not only more pay but also social advancement. I was no longer a workman in the factory, who worked for wages; I was a clerk who received a salary. I felt as people in England probably feel when peerage is conferred upon them. My fellow workers in the factory, including

Eilers, who first got me the job, showed no envy. They agreed with Jim, who told them that I was "smart." Jim used the same word which my Vila on the banks of the Delaware had used whenever I made a good recitation in English, and I saw in it a good omen. Jim and Vila and Christian of West Street were my authorities, who expressed what I considered a competent opinion upon my apprenticeship as greenhorn, and that opinion was favorable. I felt assured that the apprenticeship was soon coming to an end.

My duties as assistant to the shipping clerk were to superintend the packing of biscuits, to help address with brush and paint the boxes in which they were packed, and to see to it that they were shipped on time. A squad of some thirty girls did the packing and they seemed at first inclined to file objections whenever I found fault with their packing. They seemed to resent being bossed by an immigrant youth whose foreign accent would "stop a train," as they sometimes expressed it. I found out from Jim that the principal object of their resentment was to make me angry, because when my Serbian temper was up my accent became most atrocious and that furnished them a most hilarious amusement. I soon became convinced that my success as assistant to the shipping clerk demanded a perfect control of my temper and a speedy improvement of my accent, each of them a most difficult task.

My efforts to control my temper were frequently put to severe tests. Now and then a biscuit, well aimed, would hit me on the head, and my Serbian blood would rush to my cheeks and I would look daggers at the supposed offender. "Look at the bashibozouk," one of the girls would sing out on these occasions, and another would add: "Did you ever see such a Bulgarian atrocity?" These words were in everybody's mouth at that time and they referred to the incidents of the Balkan War of 1876–1878, which Serbia, Montenegro, and Russia were waging against the Turks. A third girl would stick her tongue out and make funny faces at me in response to my savage glare. She evidently tried to make me laugh, and I did laugh. Then a fourth girl would sing out: "Oh, look at the darling now; I just love him when he smiles." Then they all would sing:

"Smile, Michael, smile,
I love your sunny style."

I did smile, and every day I smiled more and more, after I had discovered that the girls did not really dislike me, but just loved to tease me whenever I showed any signs of a European greenhorn. I dropped the airs put on by European superiors in authority and gradually the girls became friendly and began to call me by my first name instead of mockingly addressing me as "Mister" as they addressed the old shipping clerk. "You are getting on swimmingly, my lad," said Jim one day, and he added something like this: "The girls are calling you Michael, just as they call me Jim. We are popular, my boy, but don't let this popularity mislead you into foolish notions. Just watch me; I have enjoyed this popularity for twenty years, and here I am still a bachelor, and an old bachelor at that. You have controlled your temper well, but how about controlling your heart, my lad?" Jim grinned and winked and placed his index finger in front of his forehead, as if to indicate that many a wise experience is stored in the practical head of a canny old fireman. I understood his meaning, but did I heed its warning? I knew that it contained a warning, and I suspected strongly that Jim had discovered one of my deepest secrets.

There was one girl among the thirty biscuit-packers who, in my opinion, never made a mistake in packing. I never took pains to inspect her work, and why should I when I was sure of her perfection? But I watched her and feasted my eyes upon her whenever I had spare time and was sure that nobody was observing me. She became conscious of it and every now and then she would suddenly look up and catch my admiring but cautious gaze. A bashful blush would give me away in spite of my efforts to hide my thoughts and feelings. She guessed them and she smiled as if greatly pleased and much amused, but she cleverly avoided giving me an opportunity to make a confession. I might have done it in spite of my extreme bashfulness. My note-books were full of her pictures, which I drew and signed under them her name, Jane Macnamara. Perhaps Jim had seen these pictures among my many sketches of the boiler-room and its contents, and hence his warning to me.

One Monday morning Jane did not appear at her usual place in the packing-room; her friend, another packing girl, told me that Jane had been married on the previous Saturday. I tried my best to appear as if I received the news with indifference, but failed. The girls observed a change; I neither smiled nor did I frown, but I thought a lot, and the girls seemed to take

quite an interest in my thoughtfulness, but studiously
avoided annoying me. Only now and then one of the
girls would whisper to me: "Penny for your thoughts,
Michael." Jim, I was sure, also observed the change,
but said nothing, as if he had observed nothing. One
day he introduced me to an acquaintance of his whom
he called Fred, who looked like a middle-aged man.
He had wonderful deep furrows in his face, and his
hands were large and very bony and looked as if the
daily toil had rubbed off all the superfluous flesh and
fat from them. Jim told me that Fred was far from
middle age, but barely over thirty, and that some
twelve years before he had plans and ambitions just as
big as mine, backed by at least as much brains as he
thought I had.

Fred's friends expected big things from him, said
Jim, but suddenly Fred lost his heart and married and
raised a big family of children somewhere in Jersey
City. "To-day," said Jim, "Fred is mentally just where
he was twelve years ago, and if he did not have the
contract of making the wooden packing-boxes for this
factory he would look even older than he is looking
now," and then he added, in his usual offhand manner
by way of illustration, that corn-stalks cease to grow
as soon as the ears of corn appear and all the sap of
the corn-stalk is served to the ears.

Referring to Fred's numerous children, Jim finished
his picture by saying that Fred looked like a withering corn-stalk with many small ears of corn on it, and
that he hoped that the withering corn-stalk would hold
out until the numerous ears of corn had ripened. He
admitted, however, that he himself was a withering

corn-stalk with no ears of corn at all; that his life was the other extreme from Fred's, and that neither he nor Fred had in their younger days studied and applied in practice the controlling regulators of life. Jim's sermons on self-control always hit the mark; and when, referring to his advice to me to control my temper, my heart, and my speech, I suggested that according to him life was a series of all kinds of controls difficult to manage, he answered that nothing is difficult when it becomes a habit. "Just examine my boiler-room," he said, "and you will find that everything is controlled. The centrifugal governor controls the speed of the engine; the safety-valve limits the pressure of steam; every fire has a regulator of its air draft, and every oven has a temperature indicator. I know them all and I watch their operations without knowing that I am doing it. Practice makes perfect, my lad, and perfection knows no difficulties even in a boiler-room as full of all kinds of tricks as human life is."

Jim's sermons were always short and far ahead of anything I had ever heard in the churches in Delaware City, or in Dayton, New Jersey, or in the Bowery Mission, or in any other church which up to that time I had visited in this country; and, moreover, they were not accompanied by congregational singing, which bored me. I understood why so many blacksmiths and other people of small learning made a great success as preachers in this country, whereas in my native village the priest, who prided himself upon his learning, was obliged to read those sermons only which were sent to him by the bishop of the diocese. I suggested to Jim in a jocular way to quit the boiler-room and become a preacher, and he answered that the boys and girls of the New England Cracker Factory in Cortlandt Street furnished a sufficiently large field for his religious and educational mission. Jim's assistance helped me much to let the dream about Jane fade away gradually and make room in my imagination for the dreams which I first saw at Princeton under that elm-tree in front of Nassau Hall.

The factory in Cortlandt Street was in many respects a college in which Jim was the chaplain; and it had a professor who should be mentioned here. It also had a dormitory; several of the young fellows employed in the factory lived on the top floor of the building. I was one of them, and I did not change my quarters when I was advanced to the position of assistant to the shipping clerk. Two great attractions kept me there. One was that the other fellows were out every evening visiting theatres and music-halls, so that I had the whole loft, and, in fact, the whole factory all to myself and to a chum of mine, who was much older than I in years but not in his position in the factory. His name was Bilharz, and he was the second attraction. He was the opposite to Jim and to every human being I had ever met. He knew nothing of nor did he care for the concrete or practical things of life, but always lived in dreams about things which happened centuries ago. He knew Latin and Greek and all kinds of literatures, but never made any attempts to make any use of his knowledge.

Factory work of the humblest kind was good enough for him, and I believed that he would have been satisfied to work for his board only, if pay had been refused him. He informed me once by an accidental slip of the tongue that he had studied theology at the University of Freiburg, in southern Germany, and would have become a priest if an unfortunate love-affair had not put an end to his ecclesiastical aspirations. He had no other aims when he came to America, he said, than to work for a modest living and to lead a life of profound obscurity, until the Lord called him away from this valley of tears, as he expressed it. He used a German expression and called the earth a "Thraenenthal." Although a German he spoke English well, being a finished scholar and having lived in America for a number of years, and having a memory for sound which impressed me as most remarkable. He sang like a nightingale, but only on evenings when we were all alone. Ecclesiastical music was his favorite, and during many an evening the strains of "Gloria in Excelsis Deo," "Ave Maria," and "I Know That My Redeemer Liveth" rang forth from the spacious lofts of the New England Cracker Factory and lost themselves in the silence of night among the deserted buildings of Cortlandt Street, which were alive in daytime only.

I never tired listening to his recitations of Latin and Greek poetry, although I did not understand it, and of selected passages from Shakespeare and Goethe, which I did understand. He loved the art of articulate speech and of melody, and he thought of things only that happened three thousand years ago when Homer sang and the Olympian gods guided the destinies of men, but he cared for nothing else. The steam-engine and every other kind of mechanism were to him a deadly prose which, in his opinion, Satan had invented for the purpose of leading astray the spirit of man. "They are the weapons by which people like you are keeping in slavery people like me," he said once, jokingly, referring to my interest in the boiler-room operations and to my admiration of the great captains of industry whose lives I studied and whose work I had seen and admired at the Philadelphia exposition.

I sometimes suspected that he felt alarmed by what he considered my worship of false gods, and that this impelled him to do everything he could for my redemption from heathenism. My admiration for his learning was great, but my sympathy for his misfortunes was even greater. His hands were once caught in a machine and most of his fingers had become stiff and crooked so that they looked like the talons of a falcon. His sharp features, a crooked nose and protruding eyes, supported this suggestion of a falcon, but his awkward, flat-footed walk suggested a falcon with broken wings; to say nothing of his other misfortunes which made him in spirit also a falcon with broken wings.

I felt that he knew a great deal more about the Jane incident than he cared to disclose to me. One day I referred to her as the Minnehaha of Cortlandt Street. "Minnehaha, laughing water," exclaimed Bilharz: "where did you ever get that, you boiler-room bug?" and he laughed as if he had never heard a funnier thing in his life. "From Jim, the boiler-room hermit, to Longfellow, one of the greatest of American poets, is a tremendous jump, a *salto mortale*, as they call it in a circus," said Bilharz; and then, growing more serious and thoughtful, he added something like this: "It is really wonderful what the eyes of a woman can do! They are just like the stars in the heavens, encouraging us poor mortals to aim at celestial heights. But many a sky-rocket seemed to be sailing for the stars and suddenly it found itself buried in mud. I am one of these sky-rockets," said Bilharz; "you are not, thanks to the timely intervention of a kindly divinity." He meant Jim.

Then, continuing in his usual dramatic manner, he recited in Latin an ode of Horace, in which the poet speaks of a youth trusting to the beaming countenance of his lady-love as a mariner trusting to the sunlit ripples of a calm sea who is suddenly upset by a treacherous squall and, being rescued, gratefully offers his wet garments in sacrifice to Neptune, the god of the sea. After translating the ode and explaining its meaning to me he urged me to hang my best clothes in the boiler-room as a sacrifice to Jim, the divinity which had rescued me from the treacherous waves of "Minnehaha, laughing water." "You are the luckiest of mortals, my boy," said Bilharz to me; "some day you will provoke the envy of the gods and then look out for stern Nemesis!" I did not understand the full meaning of these classical allusions, but he assured me that some day I should. I told Bilharz that my luck, of which he spoke so often, was mostly due to my being so near to a man of his learning, and that I thought he ought to be a professor in Nassau Hall at Princeton. He declined the honor, but offered to prepare me for it, and I accepted.

Bilharz was very moody and for days and days he had nothing to say to anybody, not even to me! No-

body else cared, because nobody understood him, but I
did care. When he discovered that I sincerely admired
his learning and was interested in his puzzling personality he became more communicative, sometimes almost human. His English accent was excellent, and I
asked his opinion about my accent and he assured me
with child-like frankness that it was rotten, but that
it could be fixed up if I submitted to a course of training prescribed for me by my Vila on the Delaware
farm. "I could not be your Vila, deformed as I am,"
said he, referring to his crippled fingers and to his
awkward walk, "but I will gladly be your satyr and
teach you how to imitate not only the sounds of human
language but also, if you wish it, the melodies of birds
and the chirping of bugs. The satyrs are great in that."

I knew that he could, because many an evening
while I was on the dormitory loft of the factory reading the Mayflower Compact, the Declaration of Independence, the American Constitution, Patrick Henry's
and Daniel Webster's speeches, and Lincoln's speech
at Gettysburg, Bilharz, in another part of the building,
would be imitating sounds of all kinds of birds and
bugs, after he had grown tired reciting Greek and
Latin poetry and singing ecclesiastical songs. That was
his only amusement, and he enjoyed it when he was
sure that nobody was listening; he made an exception
in my case. We finally made the start in what he
called my preparation for Nassau Hall. In the course
of less than a month I finished reciting to Bilharz the
Declaration of Independence, the American Constitution, and Lincoln's speech at Gettysburg, submitting
to many corrections and making many efforts to give

each word its proper pronunciation, and finally he accepted my performance as satisfactory.

By that time I knew these documents by heart and so did Bilharz, and he, in spite of himself, liked them so well that he accused me of conspiring to make an American out of him. "You are sinking rapidly, my boy, in the whirlpool of American democracy, and you are dragging me down with you," said Bilharz one evening, when I objected to some of the amendments which he offered in order to harmonize the American theory of freedom with the principles of German socialism. He admitted that he, a loyal Roman Catholic, did not care much for German social democracy, but that he often wondered why the American enthusiasts for democracy did not take German social democracy and save themselves the trouble of writing the Declaration of Independence. I called his attention to the fact that American democracy is much older than German social democracy, and he, somewhat irritated by that suggestion and by my defense of American democracy, as I understood it, suggested that he should resign his position as my teacher and become my pupil. His flippant criticism of American democracy and my stiff defense of it helped me much to see things which otherwise I should have missed, but these discussions threatened the entente cordiale between Bilharz and myself.

Finally we compromised and changed our course of reading, dropping things relating to political theories and taking up poetry. Longfellow's and Bryant's poetry were my favorites. "The Village Blacksmith" and "Thanatopsis" I knew by heart and enjoyed reciting to Bilharz, who was greatly pleased whenever in these recitations I avoided making a single serious break in my pronunciation. After reading some of Shakespeare's dramas which Booth and other famous actors like Lawrence Barrett and John McCullough were playing at that time, I visited the theatre often, and from my modest gallery seat I would analyze carefully the articulation of every syllable which Booth and the other actors were reciting. Booth did not have a big voice; it was much smaller than the voice of Lawrence Barrett or of powerful John McCullough, but I understood him better. Bilharz explained it by saying that Booth had a perfect articulation. "Articulation is an art which the Greeks invented; big voice is brute force common among the Russians," he used to say, protesting whenever he had an opportunity against mere physical strength, which was natural considering his scanty physical resources. He hated both the Russians and the Prussians, because, in his opinion, they both were big brutes. In those days the southern Germans had no love for the Prussians.

He never missed a single chance to sing the praises of Greek drama and of the Greek theatre and of everything which flourished during the classical age. He called my attention to the enormous size of Greek theatres and to the necessity of perfect articulation on the part of Greek actors if they were to be heard. "They were great artists," said he; "our actors are duffers only. We are all duffers! Give me the Greeks, give me Homer, Pindar, Demosthenes, Plato, Praxiteles, Phidias, Sophocles, and hundreds of others who spoke the language of the gods and did things which only the divine spirit in man can do, and you can have your Morse, McCormick, Howe, Ericsson, and the rest of the materialistic crew who ran the show at Philadelphia."

He certainly told many a fine story when he spoke of the great poets, orators, philosophers, and sculptors of Greece, and his stories impressed me much because they were great revelations to me; they were the first to arouse my interest in the great civilization of Greece. They would have impressed me even more if Bilharz had not displayed a glaring tendency to exaggerate, in order to create a strong contrast between what he called the idealism of classical Greece and what he called the realistic materialism of modern America. According to him the first had its seat among the gods on the ethereal top of Mount Olympus and the second one was sinking deeper and deeper through the shafts of coal and iron mines into the dark caverns of material earth. "No action," said Bilharz, "which needs the assistance of a steam-engine or of any other mechanism can trace its origin to idealism nor can it end in idealism." I suggested that every animal body is a mechanism and that its continuous evolution seems to indicate that the world is heading for a definite ideal. Bilharz flew up like a hornet when he heard the word evolution.

A lively discussion was going on in those days between the biological sciences and theology, Huxley and many other scientists championing the claims of Darwin's evolution theory and the theologians defending the claims of revealed religion. I was too young and too untutored to understand much of those learned discussions, but Bilharz followed them with feverish anxiety. His theological arguments did not appeal to me, and so far as I was concerned they lost even the little force they had when Bilharz turned them against what he called American mechanism and materialism, which he tried to make responsible for the alleged materialism of the evolution theory. His political and philosophical theories based upon blind prejudice created a gap between him and me which widened every day. Here are some illustrations of it.

When I described to him the election day of 1876, telling him that I and thousands of others had stood quietly and patiently hours and hours in drenching rain in front of the New York *Tribune* building waiting for the returns which would tell us whether Hayes or Tilden was to be the supreme executive head of the United States during the coming four years; how the next day some of the newspapers had raised a howl of "fraud," accusing the Republican party of tampering with the election returns in one of the States, but that the people of New York City and of the whole country had paid no attention, trusting implicitly to the machinery of government to straighten out crookedness if it existed, and how this dignity of American democracy thrilled me when I compared it with the rows and scandals accompanying elections in the countries of the military frontier of Austria-Hungary, he only laughed and ridiculed the whole procedure of electing by ignorant voters the supreme executive head of a nation. He told me a story of Aristides of Athens, who, being requested by a voter to write upon a shell the name of the man who was to be condemned for some crime which was not quite clear to the Athenian voter, wrote down his own name, and Aristides, the just, the noblest character of Athens, was condemned. But the condemnation of this just and noble and innocent man was, according to Bilharz, a condemnation of the Athenian democracy, whose shortcomings brought the downfall of Greek civilization, and he added that the shortcomings of American democracy would bring the downfall of the old European civilization.

The Aristides story interested me much, but the inference he drew from it made me think of Christian of West Street, and of his blunt remark: "A European greenhorn must have told you that." Jim was present at this discussion. He was a strong Presbyterian and ridiculed on every occasion what he called Bilharz's Roman Catholic views. This time he quoted Lincoln by saying "that government of the people, by the people, for the people, shall not perish from the earth." Then he added for the edification of Bilharz that religion in the Roman Catholic church is of the church, by the church, for the church, and that this was the real reason why Bilharz, trained in this kind of theology, would never understand American democracy. This shocked me, because I expected a fist fight between my two best friends, but . . . the fist fight did not take place.

I enjoyed taking long walks on Broadway whenever I had free time, going up on one side and coming down on the other, inspecting every window in bookstores and art stores and looking at the latest things in pictorial art, at the titles of the latest things in literature,

and at the photographs and engravings of prominent
men of the day. This gave me quite an idea of what
was going on in the American world of intellect. Bilharz never joined me because, he said, there was nothing worth seeing on these inspection tours of mine.
Once during the noon recess I managed to take him
around the corner of Cortlandt Street and Broadway
trusting to luck to meet a certain great person whom I
had seen several times before and recognized because
I saw his photograph in the shop-windows of Broadway. I succeeded, for there in the midst of the Broadway crowd appeared before us William Cullen Bryant,
the author of "Thanatopsis"! He was then the editor
of *The Evening Post,* which was located on Broadway
not far from Cortlandt Street. I pointed him out; Bilharz held his breath and, referring to the wonderful
appearance of the great poet, he said: "There is the
only man in this materialistic land of reapers and mow-
ing-machines and chattering telephone disks who could
take a seat among the gods on Mount Olympus and
be welcomed there by the shades of the great idealists
of Greece."

At another time I managed to take him as far as
City Hall; it was some holiday, and the papers had
announced that President Hayes and his secretary of
state, William Evarts, would be at City Hall at noon,
and they were there. Bilharz and I stood in a huge
crowd, but we had a good view of the President and of
his secretary of state, and we heard every word of their
short speeches. They were dressed just like everybody
else, but their remarkable physiognomies and their
scholarly words convinced me that they belonged to

the exalted position into which the vote of the people had placed them. The New York *Sun* was a bitter opponent of President Hayes and published his picture on the editorial page of every one of its issues. In this picture the letters spelling "fraud" were represented as branded across the expansive brow of the President.

But as I looked at him standing in front of City Hall and beheld the light which was reflected from his smooth and honest brow I knew that the New York *Sun* was wrong, and I vowed never to read it again until that picture disappeared from its editorial pages. Bilharz did not understand my admiration of the scene which we had witnessed: the democratic simplicity of the highest officials in the great United States and the very informal reception given to them in the great metropolis, New York, was all due, according to him, to a lack of artistic taste on the part of vulgar democracy. I thought of the multicolored uniforms loaded with shining decorations, of the plumed hats and long sabres, and of the numerous glaring flags with imperial eagles displayed on such occasions in the Austrian Empire, and I told Bilharz that if that monkey business was all due to a profusion of artistic taste, then give me the simplicity of vulgar democracy. Bilharz shrugged his shoulders and pitied me, and I pitied him for having to pass, as he assured me often, the rest of his days in this—to him—the most uninteresting part of the valley of tears, das Thraenenthal, as he called this terrestrial globe.

Such were the many differences of mental attitude which widened the gap between Bilharz and myself. He clung to the notions which were handed down to

the Old World from generations long departed; I, following Jim's suggestion, was trying to pick up where-
ever I could new ideas in the New World. Much
learning hath made him mad, thought I, whenever I
analyzed the strange ideas which Bilharz had of the
United States of America. I came to the conclusion
that his term of apprenticeship as greenhorn would
never end. It is a national calamity that the vast majority of our immigrants never see the end of their
apprenticeship as greenhorns.

I wished to believe that I was no longer a greenhorn,
and I certainly did not wish to listen to opinions of a
greenhorn such as were the opinions of Bilharz in matters outside of Greek and Roman history and of the
civilization which it described. His eyes were continu-
ally turned to a sunset the glory of which had faded
long ago; my eyes watched just as eagerly for the daily
sunrise as they did on the pasturelands of my native
village, and each sunrise showed me something new in
this—to me—still unknown land. He contemplated
the past, and I explored the present and dreamed
about the future. I thought of Jim's prophecy which
said that some day I should outgrow the opportunities
of Cortlandt Street, and I felt confident that the day
had arrived. My mind was made up to search for new
opportunities, but Jim, and Bilharz also, in spite of his
shortcomings, were still a great attraction, and I moved
slowly.

One day, after leaving Cooper Union Library, I
walked along the upper Bowery, refreshing my memories of the hard winter of 1874–1875. In Broome Street
near the Bowery I saw a store with a sign bearing the

name of Lukanitch. The man of that name must be a Serb, thought I, and I walked in, longing to hear the language which I had not heard for over three years. It was a hardware store dealing principally in files and tools made of hardened steel. Behind the desk stood an elderly man, and he, much surprised, answered my Serbian greeting in the Serbian language with an accent reminding me of Kos, my Slovene teacher in Panchevo. Lukanitch told me that he was a Slovene and that in his young days he was a pedler, a Kranyats, as they called the Slovenian pedlers in my native village. His annual summer tours took him to my native Banat.

A Kranyats travels on foot hundreds of miles, carrying on his back a huge case with numerous small drawers, each drawer containing a different line of goods: pins, needles, and threads; pens and pencils, cheap jewelry and gaily colored handkerchiefs; cotton, linen, silk, and all kinds of things which the peasants are apt to buy. A Kranyats was a familiar sight in my native village, and he was always welcome there, because he was a Slovene, a near kin to the Serb; and the Serb peasants of the Banat plains loved to hear a Kranyats describe the beauties of the mountainsides of little Slovenia on the eastern slope of the Dolomites.

When I disclosed my name to Lukanitch he asked me for my father's name, and when I told him that it was Constantine and that he lived in Idvor, Banat, his eyes looked like two scintillating stars. He gave me a big hug and a big tear threatened to roll down his cheek when he said: "Ko che ko Bog?" (Who can fathom the will of God?) After relating to me that my father had befriended him nearly thirty years prior to that time and that he had often stayed as guest at my father's house whenever his annual tours as Kranyats took him through Idvor, he begged me to come to his house on the following Sunday and dine with his family. I did, and there I met his good wife, a fine Slavonic type, and also his son and daughter, who were born in this country and who looked like young Slavs with Americanism grafted upon them. His son was about to graduate from a high school, and his daughter was preparing for Normal College. They were both American in manner and sentiment, but father and mother, although deeply devoted to the United States, the native country of their children, were still sincerely attached to the beautiful customs of the Slovene land. The children preferred to speak English, but they delighted in Slovene music, which they cultivated with much enthusiasm.

That made their parents most happy. Their home was a beautiful combination of American and Slovene civilization. Once they invited me to an anniversary party and I found the whole family dressed in most picturesque Slovenian costumes; but everybody in the party, including even old Lukanitch and his wife and all the Slovenian guests, spoke English. Most of the guests were Americans, but they enjoyed the Slovenian dishes and the Slovenian music, singing, and dancing as much as anybody. To my great surprise the American girls, friends of Miss Lukanitch, played Slovenian music exceedingly well, and I thought to myself that a sufficiently frequent repetition of parties of that kind would soon transform the American population in the

PROFESSOR PUPIN AMONG THE BOYS OF THE BERKSHIRE
INDUSTRIAL FARM

vicinity of Prince Street into Slovenians. This inter-
action between two very different civilizations gave
me food for thought, which I am still digesting mentally.

Lukanitch and his family became my devoted friends,
and they were just as interested in my plans and aspirations as if I had been a member of their family. The
old lady had a tender heart, and she shed many a tear
listening to bits of my history from the time when I
bade good-by to father and mother at the steamboat
landing on the Danube, five years before. The disappearance of my roast goose at Karlovci, my first railroad ride from Budapest to Vienna, my dialogues with
the train conductor and the gaudy station-master at
Vienna, and my free ride in a first-class compartment
from Vienna to Prague in company with American
friends amused her and her husband hugely. I had to
repeat the story many a time for the benefit of her
Slovenian friends. She begged me repeatedly to tell
the story of my crossing of the Atlantic and of my
hardships as greenhorn, being evidently anxious to have
her children hear it. I did it several times, scoring
much success on each occasion, and as a reward she
loaded me with many little gifts and with many en-
joyable feasts on Sundays and holidays.

My interpretation of the American theory of freedom, which I had derived from reading the lives and
the utterances of the great men who made this country
and from my three years' struggle as greenhorn, found
a most appreciative audience in the Lukanitch family.
They applauded Jim's sentiment, that this country is
a monument to the great men who made it, and not to
a single family like the Hapsburgs of Austria-Hungary.

Old Lukanitch offered to engage me as his teacher in American history, and young Lukanitch offered to get me an invitation from the principal of his high school to deliver an oration on the Declaration of Independence. The offers were not meant very seriously, but there was enough sincerity in them to make me believe that my training in America was recognized as having substantial value by people whose opinion deserved respect. I saw in it the first real recognition referred to in the prophecy of my fellow passenger on the immigrant ship who said: "No matter who you are or what you know or what you have, you will be a greenhorn when you land in the New World, and a greenhorn has to serve his apprenticeship as greenhorn before he can establish his claim to any recognition." I said to myself: "Here is my first recognition small as it may be, and I am certainly no longer a greenhorn."

No longer a greenhorn! Oh, what a confidence that gives to a foreign-born youth who has experienced the hardships of serving his apprenticeship as a greenhorn! Then there were other sources of confidence: I had a goodly deposit in the Union Dime Savings Bank and it was several thousand times as big as the nickel which I brought to Castle Garden when I landed. Besides, I had learned a thing or two in the evening classes at Cooper Union, and my English was considered good not only in vocabulary and grammar, but also in articulation, thanks to Bilharz. Young Lukanitch assured me that my knowledge of English, mathematics, and science would easily take me into college. He even prophesied a most successful college career, pointing at my big chest and broad shoulders and feeling my hard biceps. "You will make a splendid college oars-man," said he, "and they will do anything for you at Columbia if you are a good oarsman, even if you do not get from Bilharz so very much Greek or Latin."

At that time Columbia stood very high in rowing. One of her crews won in the Henley Regatta, and its picture could be seen in every illustrated paper. I had seen it many a time and remembered the looks of every member of that famous crew. Young Lukanitch was so enthusiastic about it that he would have gone to Columbia himself if his father had not needed him so much in his steel-tool business. He did his best to turn my eyes from Nassau Hall to Columbia. He succeeded, but not so much on account of my prospects in rowing as on account of other things, and among them was the official name of that institution: "Columbia College in the City of New York." The fact that the college was located in the city of New York carried much weight, because New York appealed to my imagination more than any other place in the world. The impression which it made upon my mind as the immigrant ship moved into New York Harbor on that clear and sunny March day when I first passed through Castle Garden, the Gate of America, never faded. My first victory on American soil was won in New York when I fought for my right to wear the red fez.

# IV

## FROM GREENHORN TO CITIZENSHIP AND
## COLLEGE DEGREE

THE Columbia boat-race victory at Henley occurred in 1878. By that time I had already with the assistance of Bilharz finished a considerable portion of my Greek and Latin preparation for Princeton—or, as I called it, for "Nassau Hall." My change of allegiance from Princeton to Columbia was gradual.

Columbia College was located at that time on the block between Madison and Park Avenues and between Forty-ninth and Fiftieth Streets in New York City. One of its proposed new buildings was, according to report, to be called Hamilton Hall, in honor of Alexander Hamilton. When I learned this I looked up the history of Alexander Hamilton. One can imagine how thrilled I was when I found that Hamilton left the junior class at Columbia College and joined Washington's armies as captain when he was barely nineteen, and at twenty was lieutenant-colonel and Washington's aide-de-camp! What an appeal to a young imagination! Few things ever thrilled me as much as the life of Alexander Hamilton. Every American youth preparing for college should read the history of Hamilton's life.

One cannot look up the history of Hamilton's life without running across the name of another great Columbia man, John Jay, first Secretary of Foreign Affairs, appointed by Congress, and the first Chief Justice of the United States, appointed by Washington, and a stanch backer of brilliant Hamilton. Chancellor Livingston, another great Columbia man, administered the first constitutional oath of office to Washington; he also completed the purchase of Louisiana from France. The more I studied the history of Hamilton's time the more I saw what tremendous influence Columbia's alumni exerted at that time. Cortlandt Street being near Trinity Church, I walked there to look at the Hamilton monument in the Trinity churchyard. This monument was the first suggestion to me of a bond of union between Trinity Church and Columbia College. Before long I found many other bonds of union between these two great institutions.

Every time I passed Columbia College in my long walks up-town and looked at the rising structure of Hamilton Hall, I thought of these three great Columbia men. What students of Hamilton's life could have looked at Hamilton Hall on Madison Avenue without being reminded of the magnificent intellectual efforts which two young patriots, Hamilton and Madison, made in the defense of the federalist form of the new American Republic? It happened thus that my memory of Nassau Hall at Princeton gradually faded, although it never vanished. The famous boat-race victory of a Columbia crew at Henley would not alone have produced this effect. It was produced by three great New York men of the Revolutionary period who were alumni of "Columbia College in the City of New York." Columbia had at that time a school of mines and engineering, separate from the college. I was much better prepared for it than for Columbia College, thanks to the evening lectures at Cooper Union, and to my natural inclination to scientific studies, but I imagined that the spirit of Hamilton, Jay, and Livingston hovered about the academic buildings of Columbia College only.

Bilharz rejoiced when I informed him of my decision to put on extra pressure in my classical studies preparatory for Columbia College, and congratulated himself, as I found out later, that he had succeeded in rescuing me from the worship of what he called scientific materialism. The good old fellow did not know that at that very time I was spending many hours of my spare time reading Tyndall's "Heat as a Mode of Motion," and Tyndall's famous lectures on Sound and Light, which he delivered in this country with great success in the early seventies.

These popular descriptions of physical phenomena were the poems in prose to which I referred before. Another book of a similar character came into my hands at that time through the Cooper Union library. I have a copy of it now, having received it over thirty years ago as a present from the late General Thomas Ewing. It is called "The Poetry of Science," published in 1848 by Robert Hunt. It starts with the following quotation from Milton:

> "How charming is Divine Philosophy!
> Not harsh and crabbed as dull fools suppose,
> But musical as is Apollo's lute
> And a perpetual feast of nectar'd sweets,
> Where no crude surfeit reigns."

Tyndall's and Hunt's writings appealed to my imagination at that time in the same way as Milton's "Paradise Lost," or as Longfellow's "Hiawatha," or as William Cullen Bryant's "Thanatopsis." They convinced me that the Slavs were not the only people who, as I had been inclined to think, see the poetical side of science, but that everybody sees it, because science on its abstract side is poetry; it is Divine Philosophy, as Milton calls it. Science is a food which nourishes not only the material but also the spiritual body of man. This was my pet argument whenever I was called upon to defend science against Bilharz's attacks.

My progress in Greek and Latin grammar under the guidance of Bilharz was rapid even before I had decided to steer for Columbia. It was a question of memory and of analysis. My memory had had a stiff linguistic training during the several years preceding that date, in trying to master the English language with all its vagaries in spelling and pronunciation. These vagaries I did not find in the grammars of the classical languages, which appeared to me to be as definite and as exact as the geometrical theorems in Euclid. Hadley's Greek Grammar did not differ much, I thought, from Davies' Legendre's Geometry. Mathematics was always my strong point, and good memory is a characteristic virtue of the Serb race; I, therefore, had an easy road in my classical studies with Bilharz.

As the time went on I saw that entrance into Columbia College was within easy reach so far as my studies were concerned. But here again the old question arose which I first asked myself three years before, when the train, taking me from Nassau Hall to the

Bowery, was approaching New York. "Social unpreparedness" stared me in the face. I could not define it, but I felt its existence. I shall try to describe it. Columbia College, a daughter of great Trinity Church, an alma mater of men like Hamilton, Jay, Livingston, and of many other gentlemen and scholars who guided the destiny of these great United States—can that great American institution, I asked myself, afford to enroll a raw Serbian immigrant among its students; train me, an uncouth employee of a cracker factory, to become one of its alumni?

I thought of the first sentence in the Declaration of Independence, but it did not persuade me that I was an equal of the American boy who was prepared to meet all the requirements necessary for entrance into Columbia College, because I was convinced that in addition to entrance examinations there were other requirements for which no prescribed examinations existed. The college of Hamilton and of Jay expected certain other things which I knew I did not have and could not get from books. A jump from the Cortlandt Street factory to Columbia College, from Jim and Bilharz to patriarchal President Barnard and the famous professors at Columbia, appeared to me like a jump over Columbia's great and venerable traditions. Old Lukanitch and his family and their American friends helped me much to start building a bridge over this big gap, but the more I associated with these people, who lived around humble Prince Street, not far from the Bowery, the more I saw my shortcomings in what I called, for want of a better name, "social preparedness." "How shall I feel," I asked myself, "when I begin to associate with boys whose parents live on Madison and Fifth Avenues, and whose ancestors were friends of Hamilton and of Jay?" Their traditions, I was sure, gave them an equipment which I did not have, unless my Serbian traditions proved to be similar to their American traditions. My native village attached great importance to traditions, and I knew how much the peasants of Idvor would resent it if a stranger not in tune with their traditions attempted to settle in their historic village.

The examination of immigrants which I saw at Castle Garden, when I landed, had made me think that traditions did not count for much in Castle Garden. But my principal acquisition from my apprenticeship as greenhorn had been the recognition that there are great American traditions, and that the opportunities of this country are inaccessible to immigrants who, like Bilharz, do not understand their meaning and their vital importance in American life. Vila's mother on the Delaware farm, my experiences with Christian of West Street, and Jim's little sermons in the Cortlandt Street boiler-room had impressed this idea upon my mind very strongly. The mental attitude of a young Serb from the military frontier was naturally very receptive to impressions of that kind. My respect for the traditions of my own race had prepared me to respect the traditions of the country which I expected to adopt, and hence I was afraid that my cultural equipment was not up to the standards of the college boys who were brought up in accordance with American traditions. My subsequent experience showed me that my anxiety was justifiable.

I have already mentioned that a short time before I ran away from Prague and headed for the United States I had read a translation of Harriet Beecher Stowe's "Uncle Tom's Cabin." It had been recommended to my by my American friends who gave me a free ride in a first-class compartment from Vienna to Prague. My mention of the name of this great woman, together with the names of Lincoln and of Franklin, as Americans that I knew something about, had won me the sympathy of the immigration officials at Castle Garden, who, otherwise, might have deported me. Her name was deeply engraved upon the tablets of my memory. The famous Beecher-Tilton trial was much discussed in those days in the New York press, and when I heard that Henry Ward Beecher was a brother of the author of "Uncle Tom's Cabin" my opinion of Tilton was formed, and no judge or jury could have changed it. Beecher's photographs, which I saw in my inspection tours on Broadway, confirmed me in my belief that he was a brother worthy of his great sister. Young Lukanitch and his sister knew of Beecher's fame and, although strict Roman Catholics, they consented to accompany me on my first pilgrimage to Beecher's Plymouth Church, and there I saw the great orator for the first time.

His face looked to me like that of a lion and his long gray locks, reaching almost to his shoulders, supported this illusion. The church provided a setting worthy of his striking appearance. The grand organ behind and above the pulpit supplied a harmonious musical background to the magnificent singing of the large choir. I felt that the thrilling music was tuning me up for the sermon which the great orator was about to preach, and I was right. The sermon was free from involved theological analysis; it dealt with simple questions of human life and its determination of human habits. It was a dramatic and poetic presentation of the little sermons which Jim preached in the Cortlandt Street boiler-room, but in a very plain form of statement. The fact, however, that I found many spiritual bonds between great Plymouth Church and Jim's humble boiler-room shows me today why Beecher touched the heart-strings of the plain people. He helped them to solve some of their problems of life just as Jim tried to help me solve mine. But Jim was not a cultured man and he delivered his chunks of practical wisdom in the same offhand manner in which he fed shovelfuls of coal to the busy fires under his boilers.

Beecher, on the other hand, was a great orator and a great poet, and every little grain of wisdom stored up in human life was placed before his congregation with all the force of his overpowering personality and with all the embellishments with which the imagination of a poetical nature could clothe it. I felt thrills creeping over my whole body as I listened, and the effect was not only mental and spiritual, but also physical, undoubtedly because of the quickening of the blood's circulation produced by the mental exhilaration. Bilharz, although a rigid Roman Catholic, admitted, after hearing Beecher several times, that great sermons are possible even without any theological flavoring. "But," said he in his usual dramatic way, "everything is possible to a poetic soul which is propelled by the wings of a genius." A remarkable concession from a man of Bilharz's training and mental attitude!

Jim, who was a strict Presbyterian, rejoiced that I had picked out a Congregational Church for religious worship, and old Lukanitch confessed that if I persuaded his children to go with me to Plymouth Church very often they might desert the Roman Catholic faith of their ancestors. I felt assured, however, that St. Sava and the Orthodoxy of my mother would never lose me through the influence of Beecher's genius, because Beecher was preaching to all humanity and not to a particular creed. His words were like the life-giving radiation of the sun, which shines upon all things alike. I saw in him a living example of that type of American who, like Hamilton, Jay, Livingston, and the other great men of whom I had heard at the Philadelphia exposition, were the spiritual and the intellectual giants of the Revolutionary period. My study of the history of Hamilton's life had shown me that the number of these giants was large; many of them signed the Declaration of Independence. I did not fail to see in this a most propitious omen of a great future for the country. What a spiritual giant Lincoln must have been, I thought, when I heard Beecher refer to him with humblest veneration! Beecher was the sunrise which dispelled much of that mist which prevented my eyes, just as it prevents all foreign eyes, from seeing the clear outline of American civilization.

Four years previously I had for the first time attended an American church service in Delaware City, and had carried away the impression that in matters of public worship America was not up to the standards prescribed by the Serbian Church. Beecher and his Plymouth Church changed my judgment completely. Beecher's congregation seemed to me like a beehive full of honey-hearted beings. Each of them reminded me of the Americans who had befriended me at the railroad-station in Vienna, and had rescued me from the official dragon who threatened to send me back to the prisons of the military frontier. I firmly believed that Beecher was preaching a new gospel, the American gospel of humanity, the same gospel which his great sister had preached. Every member of his congregation looked to me like a faithful disciple of this doctrine.

One of those honey-hearted disciples was a Doctor Charles Shepard, of Columbia Heights, Brooklyn. He and his family were Unitarians, I think, but they often attended Plymouth Church on account of their great admiration for Beecher. Doctor Shepard's family was, in my opinion, a family of saints; generosity, refinement, and spiritual discipline filled the golden atmosphere of their home. When I disclosed my plans to the good doctor, he offered to help me carry them out. He was an ardent advocate of the curative powers of hydropathy in conjunction with proper diet and total abstinence from alcohol and tobacco. "Cleanliness is next to godliness" was his motto, and by cleanliness he meant freedom from unclean habits of every kind. His theory was successfully practised in his hydropathic establishment, and he flourished, and his institution was famous.

His very old father, over eighty years of age, who managed the office of the establishment, needed assistance, and Doctor Shepard offered me the position and spoke of getting a friend of his to help me prepare for entrance to Columbia. His friend was Professor Webster, who taught Greek and Latin at the Adelphi Academy in Brooklyn. I jumped at Doctor Shepard's offer, although the prospect of deserting Jim and Bilharz made me hesitate. But Jim applauded my decision and he recalled his prophecy that I should soon outgrow the opportunities of the New England Cracker Factory. Bilharz expressed his gratification that he had contributed to my progress, and he certainly had, both by what he praised and by what he condemned. He was sincere in both, but his praise was founded upon a rare knowledge of classical literatures, while his condemnation was due to prejudice against science and against American democracy. The real secret of his grip upon my imagination I shall disclose later.

Professor Webster was an ideal pedagogue; his pupils were boys and girls from some of the best families of Brooklyn. Their teacher was to them an apostle of classical culture, in which they were much interested, partly because of their admiration for their beloved teacher. After a few private lessons he invited me to join his classes in Greek and Latin, where I was received with many signs of cordiality from both the boys and the girls. Like myself, they were preparing for college. I attended these classes three times a week and entertained them much by my continental pronunciation of Greek and Latin, which I had learned from Bilharz, who had also taught me to recite the Greek and Latin hexameter with proper intonation. This delighted the heart of Professor Webster and of his pupils. Recitations of Greek and Latin verses with

A high m
fees at Co
Shepard a
ingly, my
Rutherfor

It was a
it had no
looked aft
near it. S
ducks and
Christoph
ville, and
to let me
should ap
for a certa
on condit
part of tl
from ten t
in the aft
and she fi
fore meals
eat her ou
scheme fo
result. Sh
with more
had ever e

Moreov
specific p
his output
work hug
joiced in 1
old lady

faultless rhythm were all which at first I could offer to the entertainment of my classmates.

After a while I entertained some of them with Serbian poetry and also with Serbian kolo dancing. I made every effort to make them forget that I was a Balkan barbarian; but everybody, as if reading my thoughts, assured me that I was contributing more to the Adelphi Academy than I was getting in return. I knew better. I felt that the association with those splendid boys and girls and with Professor Webster contributed much more to my preparation for Columbia than all the book work which I had ever done anywhere.

Doctor Shepard and his family saw the rapid change in me, I thought, and many of their evidences of approval were very encouraging. When I first met Doctor Shepard he was strongly pro-Turkish whenever the Balkan war, which was raging at that time, was discussed. He had a notion that the Serbians were a rebellious and barbarous race. During the early part of 1879 he gradually shifted to the Serbian side, and I was bold enough to take all credit for it to myself. I considered his and his family's approval the best test of the success of my efforts to understand the American standards of conduct. This success meant much more to me in my preparation for college than the success in my studies.

In an interscholastic athletic contest I volunteered to run in a ten-mile race without any previous training, and won. From that day on my friends at the Adelphi Academy regarded me as one of their number, and it was a liberal education to me to listen to their eulogies

Every two-hour period of sawing and splitting of kindling-wood was followed by a dip and swim in the Passaic River, and by the end of the summer I was all muscle and could have run a race of twenty miles without any previous training. This proved a very valuable asset in the beginning of my college career; muscle and brawn are splendid things to take along when one enters college, and have while in college. Several incidents in my college career bear upon the interesting feature of athletics in American college life, and I shall describe them later even at the risk of appearing egotistical. This feautre is characteristically American and is quite unknown on the continent of Europe.

Eight hours each day I devoted to study: three in the morning to Greek, three in the afternoon to Latin, and two in the evening to other studies. It was a most profitable summer outing of over three months, and it cost me only thirty dollars; the rest was paid in sawing and splitting of kindling-wood. Whenever I read now about the Kaiser's activities at Doorn, I think of my summer activities in 1879, and I wonder who in the world suggested my scheme to William Hohenzollern!

During the last week of September of that year I presented myself at Columbia for entrance examinations. They were oral, and were conducted by the professors themselves and not by junior instructors. The first two books of the Iliad, excepting the catalogue of ships, and four orations of Cicero, I knew by heart. My leisure time at my Passaic River "villa" had permitted me these pleasant mental gymnastics; I wanted to show off before Bilharz with my Greek and Latin quotations;

to say nothing of the wonderful mental exhilaration which a young student gets from reading aloud and memorizing the words of Homer and of Cicero. The professors were greatly surprised and asked me why I had taken so much trouble. I told them that it was no trouble, because Serbs delight in memorizing beautiful lines. The Serbs of Montenegro, for instance, know by heart most of the lines which their great poet Nyegosh ever wrote, and particularly his great epic "The Mountain Glory." I told them also of illiterate Baba Batikin, the ministrel of my native village, who knew most of the old Serbian ballads by heart.

Besides, I assured the professors, I wanted to do in Greek and Latin as well as I possibly could, so as to gain free tuition. For the other studies I was not afraid, I told them, and they assured me that my chances for free tuition were certainly good. The other examinations gave me no trouble, thanks to my training with Bilharz and with the lecturers in the evening classes at Cooper Union. A note from the Registrar's office informed me a few days later that I was enrolled as a student in Columbia College with freedom from all tuition fees. There was no person in the United States on that glorious day happier than I!

The college atmosphere which I found at Columbia at that time gave me a new sensation. I did not understand it at first and misinterpreted many things. The few days preceding the opening of the college sessions I spent chasing around for a boarding-house, while my classmates were hanging around the college buildings, making arrangements to join this or that fraternity, and also solidifying the line of defense of the freshmen against the hostile sophomores. There was a lively process of organization going on under the leadership of groups of boys who came from the same preparatory schools. These groups led and the others were expected to follow without a murmur. Insubordination or even indifference was condemned as lack of college spirit. This spirit was necessary among the freshmen particularly, because, as I was informed later, there was a great common danger—the sophomores!

I saw some of this feverish activity going on, but did not understand its meaning and hence remained outside of it, as if I were a stranger and not a member of the freshman class, which I heard described, by the freshmen themselves, as the best freshman class in the history of Columbia. The sophomores denied this in a most provoking manner; hence the hostility. Nobody paid any attention to me; nobody knew me, because I did not come from any of the preparatory schools which prepared boys for Columbia.

One day I saw on the campus two huge waves of lively youngsters beating against each other just like inrolling waves of the sea lifting on their backs the returning waves which had been reflected from the cliffs of the shore. The freshmen were defending a cane against fierce attacks of the sophomores. It was the historic Columbia cane rush, I was told by Michael, the college janitor, who stood alongside of me as I looked on. It was not a real fight resulting in broken noses or blackened eyes, but just a most vigorous push-and-pull contest, the sophomores trying to take possession of a cane which a strong freshman, surrounded by a stalwart body-guard of freshmen, was holding and guarding just as a guard of fanatic monks would defend the sacred relics of a great saint.

This freshmen group was the centre of the scrimmage and it stood there like a high rock in the midst of an angry sea. Coats and shirts were torn off the backs of the brave fighters, some attacking and others defending the central group, but not a single ugly swear-word was heard nor did I see a single sign of intentional bloodshed. Members of the junior and senior classes watched as umpires. Michael, the janitor, who knew everybody on the college campus as a shepherd knows his sheep, was not quite certain about my identity. He asked me whether I was a freshman, and when I said "yes," he asked me why in the world I was not in the rush, defending the freshmen body-guard. He looked so anxious and worried that I felt sure of being guilty of some serious offense against old Columbia traditions.

I immediately took off my coat and stiff shirt and plunged into the surging waves of sophomores and freshmen and had almost reached the central body-guard of freshmen, eager to join in its defense, when a sophomore, named Frank Henry, grabbed me and pulled me back, telling me that I had no business to cross the line of umpires at that late moment. I did not know the rules of the game and shoved him aside and we clinched. He was the strongest man in Columbia College, as I learned later, but my kindling-wood operations on the banks of the Passaic River had made me a stiff opponent. We wrestled and wrestled and would have wrestled till sunset like Prince Marco and the Arab Moussa Kessedjia in the old Serbian ballads, if the umpires had not proclaimed the cane rush a draw.

The main show being over, the side show which Henry and I were keeping up had no further useful purpose to serve, and we stopped and shook hands. He was glad to stop, he admitted, and so was I, but he told my classmates that "if that terrible Turk had been selected a member of the freshmen body-guard the result of the cane rush might have been different." I told him that I was a Serb, and not a Turk, and he apologized, saying that he could never draw very fine distinctions between the various races in the Balkans. "But, whatever race you are," said he, "you will be a good fellow if you will learn to *play the game*." Splendid advice from a college boy! *"Play the game,"* what a wonderful phrase! I studied it long, and the more I thought about it the more I was convinced that one aspect of the history of this country with all its traditions is summed up in these three words.

No foreigner can understand this country who does not know the full meaning of this phrase, which I first heard from a Columbia College youngster. No foreign language can so translate the phrase as to reproduce its brevity and at the same time convey its full meaning. But, when I heard it, I thought of the bootblacks and newsboys who, five years previously, had acted as umpires when I defended my right to wear a red fez. To "play the game" according to the best traditions of the land which offered me all of its opportunities was always my idea of Americanization. But how many immigrants to this land can be made to understand this?

Some little time after this incident I was approached by the captain of the freshman crew, who asked me to join his crew. I remembered young Lukanitch's opinion about oarsmanship at Columbia, and I was sorely tempted. But, unfortunately, I had only three hundred and eleven dollars when I started my college career, and I knew that if I was to retain my free tuition by high standing in scholarship and also earn further money for my living expenses I should have no time for other activities. "Study, work for a living, no participation in college activities outside of the recitation-room! Do you call that college training?" asked the captain of the freshman crew, looking perfectly surprised at my story, which, being the son of wealthy parents, he did not understand.

I admitted that it was not, in the full sense of the word, but that I was not in a position to avail myself of all the opportunities which Columbia offered me, and that, in fact, I had already obtained a great deal more than an immigrant could reasonably have expected. I touched his sympathetic chord, and I felt that I had made a new friend. The result of this interview was that my classmates refrained from asking me to join any of the college activities for fear that my inability to comply with their request might make me feel badly. I had their sympathy, but I missed their fellowship, and therefore I missed in my freshman year much of that splendid training outside of the classroom which an American college offers to its students.

At the end of the freshman year I gained two prizes of one hundred dollars each, one in Greek and the

had held his own against experienced mowers in the Hackensack meadows. The victory was quick and complete, and my classmates carried me in triumph to Fritz's saloon, not far from the college, where many a toast was drunk to "Michael the Serbian." From that day on my classmates called me by my first name and took me up as if I had been a distinguished descendant of Alexander Hamilton himself.

My scholastic victory in Greek and mathematics meant nothing to my classmates, because it was a purely personal matter, but my athletic victory meant everything, because it was a victory of my whole class. Had I won my scholastic victory in competition with a representative from another college, then the matter would have had an entirely different aspect. *Esprit de corps* is one of those splendid things which American college life cultivates, and I had the good fortune to reap many benefits from it. He who pays no attention to this *esprit de corps* in an American college runs the risk of being dubbed a "greasy grind."

The sophomore year opened auspiciously. Eight of my classmates formed a class, the Octagon, and invited me to coach them in Greek and in mathematics, twice a week. The captain of the class crew was a member of it. I suspected that he remembered my reasons for refusing to join the freshman crew and wanted to help. The Octagon class was a great help in more ways than one. I gave instruction in wrestling also to several classmates, in exchange for instruction in boxing. This was my physical exercise, and it was a strenuous one. Devereux Emmet, a descendant of the great Irish patriot, was one of these exchange instructors; he could stand any amount of punishment in our boxing bouts, which impressed upon my mind the truth of the saying that "blood will tell."

Before the sophomore year was over my classmates acknowledged me not only a champion in Greek and in mathematics, but also a champion in wrestling and boxing. The combination was somewhat unusual and legends began to be spun about it, but they did not turn my head, nor lull me to sleep, not even when they led to my election as class president for the junior year. This was indeed a great compliment, for, because of the junior promenade, the dance given annually by the junior class, it was customary to elect for that year a class president who was socially very prominent. A distinguished classmate, a descendant of three great American names, and a shining light in New York's younger social set, was my chief opponent and I begged to withdraw in his favor; a descendant of Hamilton inspired awe.

But my opponent would not listen to it. He was a member of the most select fraternity and not at all unpopular, but many of my classmates objected to him, although he was the grandson of a still living former Secretary of State and chairman of the board of trustees of Columbia College. They thought that he paid too much attention to the fashion-plates of London, and dressed too fashionably. There were other Columbia boys at that time who, I thought, dressed just as fashionably, and yet they were very popular; but they were fine athletes, whereas my opponent was believed to rely too much upon the history of his long name and upon his splendid appearance. He certainly

presently I saw a flock of lame ducks gathering around me, offering liberal rewards for a speedy cure. My summer vacations no longer called me to the Passaic River to cut kindling-wood, nor to the Hackensack meadows to strain my back to the utmost trying to keep up with experienced mowers. Coaching lame ducks was incomparably more remunerative and also left me with plenty of leisure time for tennis, horse-back riding, or swimming and diving contests.

During the college sessions I usually had in charge several bad cases of academic lameness, cases that could not be cured during the summer vacations, but had to be carefully nursed throughout the whole academic year. Financially I fared better than most of my young professors, and I saved, looking ahead for the realization of a pet dream of mine. My coaching experience was remunerative not only from the material but also from the cultural side; it brought me in touch with some of the best exponents of New York's social life, where I found a hearty welcome, a friendly sympathy, and many lessons which I considered as among the most valuable acquisitions in my college life. One of them deserves special mention here.

Lewis Morris Rutherfurd, a trustee of Columbia College, was at that time the head of the famous Rutherfurd family. He was a gentleman of leisure and devoted himself to science and particularly to photographic astronomy, just as did his famous friend, Doctor John William Draper, the author of the "History of the Intellectual Development of Europe." Rutherfurd was a pioneer worker in this field of astronomy, and his photographs of the moon and of the stars were always regarded by the scientists of the world as most valuable contributions to astronomy. The historic Rutherfurd mansion, with its astronomical observatory, was on Eleventh Street and Second Avenue. Rutherfurd's sons, Lewis and Winthrop, were my fellow students at Columbia; Lewis was a year ahead of me and Winthrop was a year below me. Through their cousin, a chum and classmate of mine, I became acquainted with them. No handsomer boys ever sat in Hamilton Hall: tall, athletic, and graceful, just like two splendid products of the physical culture of classical Greece. One of them held the American championship in racquets, and the Long Island hunt clubs counted them among their best steeplechase riders. Lewis just squeezed his way through college, but Winthrop, owing to circumstances beyond his control, threatened to drop by the academic roadside; the load of some seven conditions was too heavy and too discouraging.

My chum, Winthrop's cousin mentioned above, was a brilliant raconteur, and he used to spin out with wonderful skill many a funny tale about my coaching experiences, describing in a grotesque manner how an audacious youngster, straying over here from a Serbian peasant village, was bullying young aristocrats of New York, and how these aristocrats were submitting to it like little lambs. Rutherfurd, senior, who was my chum's uncle, heard some of these humorous tales. He enjoyed them hugely, and they suggested to him a scheme for diminishing somewhat his son's heavy load of conditions. He and his family were to spend the summer of 1882 in Europe, and he suggested that Win-

manly American youth whose friendship I was proud to possess.

In the autumn Winthrop got rid of most of his conditions, proceeded with his class, and eventually graduated from Columbia in 1884. My imaginative chum, Winthrop's cousin, composed a great tale describing this incident and called it: "A Serbian Peasant versus an American Aristocrat." Those who had the good fortune to enjoy the humor of this tale (and among them was F. Marion Crawford, the novelist and cousin of my chum) pronounced it a great literary accomplishment, and they all agreed that Winthrop was the real hero of the story; he had played the game like a thoroughbred. Mr. Rutherfurd, senior, enjoyed the tale as much as anybody, and he was delighted with the result of our summer work. Winthrop's behavior did not surprise him, because, he assured me, Winthrop played the game as every American gentleman's son would have played it. "Every one of your classmates," exclaimed this trustee of Columbia College, "would have done the same thing; or he would be unworthy of a Columbia degree." The first function of the American college, according to him, was to train its students in the principles of conduct becoming an American who is loyal to the best traditions of his country.

My senior year opened even more auspiciously than my sophomore or my junior year had. Lewis Rutherfurd, trustee of Columbia College, gentleman and scholar, and famous scientist, become my mentor. Winthrop's success was to place him under very great obligations to me, he had said before he sailed for Europe in the spring, and after his return his actions proved that he had meant even more than he had said. A father could not have been more solicitous about my future plans than he was, and his advice indicated that he understood my case much better than I did myself. At the beginning of my senior year I was still undecided as to what I was to do after graduation, and I began to feel anxious; my mentor's advice was most welcome, and it certainly was one of the determining factors of my future plans.

In my preceding account of my preparations for college and of my life in college there is much which sounds like a glorification of muscle and of the fighting spirit. I feel almost like apologizing for it, but do I really owe an apology? My whole life up to this point of my story was steered by conditions which demanded muscle and the fighting spirit. To pass six weeks during each one of several summers as herdsman's assistant in company with twelve other lively Serb youngsters as fellow assistants, meant violent competitions in wrestling, swimming, herdsman's hockey, and other strenuous games for hours and hours each day, and one's position in this lively community depended entirely upon muscle and the fighting spirit. Magyarism in Panchevo and Teutonism in Prague produced a reaction which appealed to muscle and to the fighting spirit, which finally drove me to the land of Lincoln. Muscle and the fighting spirit of the bootblacks and newsboys on Broadway met me on the very first day when I ventured to pass beyond the narrow confines of Castle Garden, in order to catch my first glimpse of the great American metropolis.

No sooner had I finished serving my apprenticeship as greenhorn, and advanced to a higher civic level, than I encountered again muscle and the fighting spirit of the college boys. In the beginning of my college career I found very little difference between the pasture-lands of my native village and the campus of the American college. The spirit of playfulness and the ferment of life in the hearts of youth were the same in both, and were manifested in the same way, namely, in athletics which encourage a glorification of muscle and of the fighting spirit. This was most fortunate for me, because it offered me a wide avenue by which I could enter with perfect ease into that wonderful activity called college life. Other avenues existed, but to a Serbian youth who but a few years before had been a herdsman's assistant these other avenues were practically closed. I have described the avenue which was open to me, but with no intention to indulge in an egotistical glorification of that avenue.

Rutherfurd, my mentor, scholar, scientist, and trustee of Columbia College, did not believe as some people do that athletics would ever cause our colleges to degenerate into gladiatorial schools. Athletics in the form of wrestling and boxing did not interfere in the least with my scholarship. Healthy young people and healthy young nations are prone to worship the heroic element in human life, thought trustee Rutherfurd, and, according to him, the Greeks, by the art of physical culture, prevented this exuberance of youth from degenerating into brutality. He was longing forty years ago, and I am still longing to-day, for the time when American colleges will have a four years' course in physical culture, conducted by medical and athletic experts. His sons, he thought, practised this art by their devotion to the game of racquets and of steeple-chase riding. They were splendid athletes, but nevertheless they were mellow-hearted and gentle youths. The fact that their scholarship was not high did not disturb their learned father, because much of his own scholarship and scientific learning, he told me, had been acquired long after he had graduated from Williams College.

Many of my fellow students were, just like myself, very fond of athletics and of other activities outside of the college curriculum, and yet we were enthusiastic students of Greek literature, of history and economics, of constitutional history of the United States, and of English literature. But here was the secret: Professor Merriam was a wonderful expounder of the great achievements of Greek civilization; Professor Monroe Smith made every one of us feel that history was an indispensable part of our daily life; Professor Richmond Mayo-Smith made us believe that political economy was one of the most important subjects in the world; and Professor Burgess' lectures on the Constitutional History of the United States made us all imagine that we understood the spirit of 1776 just as well as Hamilton did.

These professors were the great scholars of Columbia College when I was a student there, and they had most attractive personalities too. The personality of the professors, like that of the famous Van Amringe, and their learning, like that of the venerable President Barnard, were the best safeguards for students who

boiler-room demonstrations supplemented by Cooper Union lectures on heat; by Tyndall's and Hunt's poetic descriptions of scientific achievements; and above all by his own visions concerning physical phenomena on the pasture-lands of his native village— that lad goes through college, and the story of his college career is nearly closed without saying anything about his scientific studies at Columbia College! That certainly looks strange, and suggests the inference that after all Bilharz had finally succeeded in tearing me away completely from what he called the worship of scientific materialism. Bilharz did not succeed in that, but what he actually did is worth relating here.

After my departure from Cortlandt Street, Bilharz felt quite lonesome and tried to get companionship and consolation from a Tyrolean zither which he managed well in spite of his stiff fingers. Knowing my fondness for Homer's heroic verse and for the lyric verse in the chorus of Greek dramas, he practised reciting them with zither accompaniment. He thus imitated most successfully a Serbian guslar's recitations of old Serbian ballads, accompanied by the single-string instrument, called *gusle*. In recognition of the success of his clever scheme, which, I was sure, he had devised for my special benefit, I called him the Greek guslar. He who has seen huge multitudes of Serbs assembled around a blind guslar in the midst of some great festive gathering, listening by the hour in spellbound silence to his recitations, will understand how Bilharz managed to attract me to many a neighborhood gathering on the top loft of the Cortlandt Street factory.

Every time I listened to the zither accompanying

his chanting of familiar Greek verses I imagined that Baba Batikin's spirit was transferred from the little peasant village of Idvor to the great metropolis of America! Whenever I told him that, he seemed to be immensely pleased, because the life of a blind guslar appealed to him much. Professor Merriam was certainly a great Greek scholar, but Bilharz was a great Greek guslar, and when he chanted the verses of the Iliad with zither accompaniment I was tempted to imagine that he was a reincarnation of Homer. Between Bilharz and Merriam I could not help devoting much of my time in college to the study of Greek. I have never regretted it, but I do regret that the academic halls of the American colleges of to-day do not resound any more with that solemn Greek rhythm which I first heard on the top loft of the Cortlandt Street factory. Bilharz disappeared from Cortlandt Street a short time before I graduated, and he left me his zither as a souvenir, and also an old edition of Homer's Iliad by the famous German philologist Dindorf. I have not seen him since that time, but I shall never forget him. He was the first to call my attention to an old and magnificent civilization, the spiritual beauty of which appealed to my young imagination with increasing force as my knowledge of it increased. I often recall his almost fanatical dislike of mechanisms, and wonder what he would say to-day if he heard the pianola, the phonograph, and some of the distortions of radio broadcasting, to say nothing of the dramatic atrocities of the kinematograph!

On the other hand, the growth of my understanding from the first day of my landing at Castle Garden was due to my feeding upon the spiritual food offered to me daily by a civilization in which I was living, and which I wished to understand but did not understand. My preparation for college lifted here and there the mist which prevented my vision from seeing the clear outline of American civilization. Columbia College brought me into touch with the college life of American boys and with men of great learning and wonderful personalities, and they helped me to dispel every particle of that mist, and there in the clear sunshine of their learning I saw the whole image of what I believed to be American civilization: a beautiful daughter of a beautiful mother, which is the Anglo-Saxon civilization. The memory of this vision always recalled to my mind the ode of Horace which opens with the line:

"O matre pulchra filia pulchrior!"

The study and the contemplation of these two civilizations, the ancient civilization of Greece and the new civilization of the Anglo-Saxons, which appealed to me as the two greatest civilizations of human history, made every other study in my college curriculum appear insignificant, although I gained several prizes in the exact sciences, and although I never gave up the idea that my future work would be in the field of science.

But there is another and perhaps the most potent reason why science figures so little in the preceding part of the story of my college career. Instruction in the exact sciences in those days was most elementary, not only at Columbia College but also in most American colleges. For instance, laboratory work in physics and in chemistry was not a part of the Columbia College curriculum, and the lecture-room told me less about physics than I had known from my studies of Tyndall's popular publications and from the Cooper Union instruction before I entered college. The question "What is Light?" I brought with me from the pasture-lands of my native village, and the professor of physics at Columbia College offered no answer to it except to refer to vibrations in an ether, the physical properties of which he admitted he could not satisfactorily describe. On this point he did not seem to be much wiser than my humble teacher Kos in Panchevo. My mentor, Rutherfurd, was always interested in this question, as in many other advanced questions in science, and he took much delight in discussing them with me. He was the first to inform me that the great question, "What is Light?" would probably be answered when we understood more clearly a new electrical theory advanced by a Scotch physicist, Maxwell by name, who was a pupil of the great Faraday.

One day toward the end of my senior year I told my mentor, Rutherfurd, of a lecture-room experiment performed by Rood, his friend, at that time professor of physics at Columbia College. This experiment was the first announcement to me that Faraday was one of the great discoverers in electrical science. The experiment was simplicity itself, and consisted of a loose coil of copper wire, held in the left hand of the lecturing professor, the terminals of the coil being connected to a galvanometer supported on the wall of the lecture-room, so that its needle could be seen by every student in the room.

When Rood, like a magician manipulating a wand, moved with his right hand a small magnet toward the coil, the distant galvanometer needle, impelled by a force which up to that time was a mystery to me, swung violently in one direction, and when the magnet was moved away from the coil the galvanometer needle swung just as violently in the opposite direction. When one terminal, only, of the coil was connected to the galvanometer, and thus the electric circuit of the coil was broken, the motion of the magnet produced no effect. *"This is Faraday's discovery of Electromagnetic Induction,"* said Rood with a deep sigh, and ended the lecture without any further comment, as if he wished to give me a chance to think it over before he added additional information. Rutherfurd knew Rood's picturesque mannerism, and my description of the experiment amused him. He suggested that the good professor was very fond of mystifying his students. I certainly was much mystified and did not wait for the next lecture to clear the mystery, but spent all day and most of the night reading about Faraday's wonderful discovery. It was made over fifty years before that time, but I had never known anything about it, although Edison's dynamos in his New York Pearl Street station had been supplying for over a year thousands of customers with electric power for incandescent lighting. Columbia College was not one of these customers for a long time after my graduation. When I finished my description of the experiment, and assured Rutherfurd that it was the most thrilling physical phenomenon that I had ever seen, and that I had remained awake almost all night after seeing it, he

looked pleased, and informed me that this very phenomenon was the basis of Maxwell's new Electrical
Theory.

That was the experiment which helped me to de-
cide a very weighty question. Professor Rood had informed me that in recognition of my high standing in
science as well as in letters I could choose either of
two graduate fellowships, one in letters or one in science, each worth five hundred dollars a year. Either
would have meant an additional three years of graduate study at Columbia. I was much tempted to turn to
letters and continue my work with Merriam, the idol
of all Columbia College students, including myself,
who had felt the wonderful charm of his personality
and of his profound and at the same time most picturesque classical scholarship.

But the magic experiment which had told me the
first story of Faraday's great discoveries, and had
aroused my dormant enthusiasm for physics, caused
me to bid good-by to Merriam and turn to science, my
first love. Nevertheless, I did not accept the fellowship in science and stay three years longer at Columbia;
I preferred to take up the study of Faraday and of Maxwell in the United Kingdom, where these two great
physicists were born and where they had made their
great discoveries. Trustee Rutherfurd and his young
nephew, my chum and classmate, John Armstrong
Chanler, applauded my decision, and promised to assist me in my undertaking whenever assistance should
be needed. Rutherfurd assured me that I should certainly succeed as well in my scientific studies in European universities as I had succeeded in my general cul-

tural studies at Columbia College, if the revelations of the new world of physics, certainly in store for me, could arouse in me the same enthusiasm which had been aroused by the revelations of that new spirit and that new current of thought which had given birth to the American civilization. That this enthusiasm would not be wanting was amply demonstrated, he said, by the effect which Faraday's fundamental experiment had produced in my imagination.

Professor Burgess, my teacher in constitutional history, had assured me, toward the end of the senior year, that I was fully prepared for American citizenship, and I had applied for my naturalization papers. I received them on the day before I was graduated. Two ceremonies which are recorded in my life as two red-letter days took place on two successive days; it is instructive to give here a brief comparison between them. The ceremony which made me a citizen of the United States took place in a dingy little office in one of the municipal buildings in City Hall Park. I received my diploma of Bachelor of Arts in the famous old Academy of Music on Fourteenth Street on the following day. There was nobody in the naturalization office to witness the naturalization ceremony except myself and a plain little clerk. The graduation ceremonies in the Academy of Music were presided over by the venerable President Barnard; his luxuriant snowy-white locks and long beard, and his luminous intelligence beaming from every feature of his wonderful face, gave him the appearance of Moses, as Michael Angelo represents him; and the academy was crowded with a distinguished and brilliant audience.

The little clerk in the office handed me my naturalization papers in an offhand manner, thinking, apparently, of nothing but the fee due from me. President Barnard, knowing of my high standing in the graduating class and of my many struggles to get there, beamed with joy when he handed me my diploma amidst the applause of my numerous friends in the audience.

When I left the naturalization office, carrying my precious multicolored and very ornate naturalization papers, the crowd in City Hall Park was moving about as though nothing had happened; but when I stepped down from the academy stage, with my Columbia diploma in hand, my old friend Doctor Shepard handed me a basket of roses with the best wishes of his family and of Henry Ward Beecher; Mr. and Mrs. Lukanitch were there, and the old lady kissed me, shedding tears copiously and assuring me that if my mother were there to see how well I looked in my academic silk gown she also would have shed many a tear of joy; numerous other friends were there and made much fuss over me, but all those things served only to increase the painful contrast between the gay commencement ceremonies and the prosy procedure of my naturalization on the preceding day. One ceremony made me only a Bachelor of Arts. The other made me a citizen of the United States. Which of the two should have been more solemn?

There was a picture which I had conjured up in my imagination when first I walked one day from the Cortlandt Street factory to Wall Street to see the site of old Federal Hall. The picture was that of Chancellor Livingston administering the constitutional oath of office to President Washington. To me it was a picture of the most solemn historical act which New York or any other place in the world ever had witnessed. When the little clerk in the naturalization office handed me my naturalization papers, and called upon me in a perfunctory way to promise that I would always be loyal to the Constitution of the United States, the picture of that historical scene in Federal Hall suddenly reappeared to me, and a strange mental exaltation made my voice tremble as I responded: "I will, so help me God!" The little clerk noticed my emotion, but did not understand it, because he did not know of my long-continued efforts throughout a period of nine years to prepare myself for citizenship of the United States.

As I sat on the deck of the ship which was taking me to the universities of Europe, and watched its eagerness to get away from the busy harbor of New York, I thought of the day when, nine years before, I had arrived on the immigrant ship. I said to myself: "Michael Pupin, the most valuable asset which you carried into New York harbor nine years ago was your knowledge of, and profound respect and admiration for, the best traditions of your race . . . the most valuable asset which you are now taking with you from New York harbor is your knowledge of, and profound respect and admiration for, the best traditions of your adopted country."

# V

## FIRST JOURNEY TO IDVOR IN ELEVEN YEARS

IT was a beautiful June afternoon when from the gay deck of the *State of Florida* I saw the low coast-line of Long Island disappear in the distance. With it disappeared the land the first glimpse of which I had caught so eagerly on that sunny March morning nine years before, when the immigrant ship *Westphalia* carried me into New York harbor. As I had approached this coast my busy imagination had suggested that it was the edge of the cover of a great and mysterious book which I had to read and decipher. I had read it for nine long years, and my belief that I had deciphered it made me confident that I was quite rich in learning. Besides, there were my Bachelor of Arts diploma and my naturalization papers; and, of course, I thought, they were the best evidence in the world that I was returning to see my mother again rich in learning and in academic honors, as I had promised her nine years before in that letter from Hamburg.

The sky was clear, the sea was smooth, and its sharp and even horizon line toward which the ship was heading promised a peaceful temper of the powers which controlled the motions of the air above and of the waters below our ship. The comforts of the ship and the fair prospects of a fine voyage were recorded in the smiling faces of my fellow passengers. A group of lively

schoolgirls from Washington, making their first trip to
Europe under the guidance of an old professor with
long gray hair and shaggy beard, looked like so many
nymphs playing around a drowsy Neptune. They
formed the central group of the happy passengers.
There were a number of college boys on board. Some
of them had friends among the Washington nymphs;
by clever manœuvring it was arranged that the college
boys, including myself, should sit at the same table
with the playful nymphs. The graylocked professor,
whom I called Father Neptune (and the title stuck to
him), was somewhat reluctant at first, but finally he
gave his consent to this "wonderful" proposition, as
the girls called it, and he sat at the head of the table,
presiding with a dignity which fully demonstrated that
he deserved the title "Father Neptune." The jolly
captain assured us that his good old ship never carried
a more exuberant company of youngsters across the
Atlantic.

But this was not the fierce Atlantic which I had seen
nine years before. It was an Atlantic which apparently
studied to please and to amuse. All kinds of pleasant
things happened during the voyage, as if arranged purposely for our amusement. Many schools of porpoises
approached the merry ship, and I suggested that they
visited us in order to pay their respects to Father
Neptune and his beautiful nymphs. This suggestion
was accepted with vociferous acclamation, and it was
agreed that free play be granted to our imaginations.
Let your fancy take any course at your own risk, was
our motto. When the visiting porpoises hustled off like
a squadron of reconnoitring horsemen leaping gaily

over the smooth waves, as if in a merry steeplechase, it
was suggested by one of the girls with a lively imagination that they were anxious to report to the chief of
staff of a great host which, hidden in the depths of the
quiescent Atlantic, controlled the ocean waves. She,
the oracle, as we called her, prophesied that when these
heralds had delivered the report that Father Neptune
and his fair nymphs were passing in triumphal procession through their watery realm, then all things in the
heavens above and in the sea below would bow to the
will of Neptune and his playful crew.

Two spouting whales appeared one day in the distance, and our busy imaginations suggested that they
were two men-o'-war, sent by the friendly submarine
host to pay their homage to Neptune and his nymphs,
and to serve as escort to our speedy ship. Nothing happened which did not receive a fanciful interpretation
by our playful imaginations. The wonderful phosphor-
escence of the waves, which were ploughed up in the
smooth sea by the gliding ship, supported the illusion
that our voyage was a triumphal procession along an
avenue illuminated by the mysterious phosphorescent
glow.

We were headed for Scotland, by a route which
passed to the north of Ireland, and as our course approached the northern latitudes the luminous twilights
of the North Atlantic made us almost forget that there
ever was such a thing as a dark night. Good old Neptune had quite a job to round up his nymphs in the
late hours of the evening and make them turn in and
exchange the joys of the busy days for the blessings
of the restful nights. His job was hopeless when the

northern midnights displayed the awe-inspiring streamers of the northern lights, and that happened quite
frequently.

Those wonderful sights in themselves would have
made it worth while crossing the Atlantic. On such
evenings the exuberance of the college boys and of the
schoolgirls from Washington was wide awake until after midnight, watching the luminous and continuously
changing streamers of the polar regions, telling stories,
and singing college songs. These evenings reminded me
much of the neighborhood gatherings in Idvor. One of
them was devoted to original stories; each member of
the gay party had to spin out an original tale. My
story was called "Franciscus of Freiburg," and it referred to Bilharz, the Greek guslar of Cortlandt Street.
The disappointments of his youth, the calm resignation
with which in his more mature years he passed his
hermit days on a top loft in Cortlandt Street, and his
search for consolation in the poetry of Rome and
Greece made quite an impression; and to my great surprise there was not a single giggle on the part of the
irrepressible nymphs.

This was the first story that I ever composed, and
it made a hit, but its success was completely ruined
when, prompted by modesty, I suggested that any tale
describing disappointments in love is sure to be taken
very seriously and sympathetically by young girls. A
violent protest was filed by the girls, and I pleaded
guilty of the offense of disturbing public peace. A
mock trial, with Father Neptune as the presiding judge,
condemned me and imposed the fine that I tell at once,
and without preparation, another original tale. I de-

scribed the first speech of my life on St. Sava's day, some thirteen years earlier, and its unexpected effect upon my mischievous chums in Idvor, comparing it with the unexpected effect of my Franciscus story. I regretted it, because the fairies from Washington had an endless chain of questions about Idvor and my prospective visit to it. Never before had I had a better opportunity to observe the beautiful relationship between American boys and girls. Its foundation I recognized to be the idea of the big brother looking after the safety, comfort, and happiness of his sister, the same idea which is glorified in the Serbian national ballads.

One pleasant incident followed another in quick succession during our triumphant procession over the northern Atlantic, and all the powers which control the temper of the ocean were most kind and generous to us, just as our fair oracle had prophesied it. When the cliffs of Scotland hove in sight, reminding us that our voyage was approaching its end, there was no thrill of joy such as there was when the immigrant ship, which first took me into New York harbor, approached the Long Island coast. Not even the countless sea-gulls which gracefully circled around the black cliffs, and with their shrill notes welcomed us to the hospitable shores of Scotland, were able to dispel the gloom which the sight of land produced among the members of Neptune's table. Nobody in our congenial company seemed to be anxious to say good-by to the good old ship and to the golden atmosphere of the sweet-tempered Atlantic. Most of them had never crossed the Atlantic before, and since the voyage was practically over I thought that there was no harm in describing to them some of the terrors of the Atlantic, which I had experienced when I crossed it nine years before.

The pictures of those experiences were like the pictures from another world, and not from the same Atlantic which thrilled us with its sunshine, twilight, phosphorescent glows, and glorious streamers of the northern lights. The comparison between my wretched fellow passengers on the storm-tossed immigrant ship and the radiant company on the ship which brought us to Scotland afforded me a splendid opportunity to thank Father Neptune for permitting me to join his beautiful court. His favor, I said, was almost as great as the favor of the immigrant officials at Castle Garden, who had allowed me to land with only five cents in my pocket.

The professor complimented me upon my word pictures which showed the glaring contrasts between the two voyages, and then he referred to two pictures which, he said, he had in his mind. They also showed, he said, in glaring contrasts, the difference between a certain youngster on the immigrant ship to which I referred, and a Columbia College graduate, who had contributed his share to the comfort and happiness of Neptune's court. When he suggested that he would give much to be with me when I met my mother, and that he wondered whether she would recognize me, my young friends suggested, quite seriously, that they would all go to Idvor if I joined them in their continental tour. I replied that their tour was along a meandering line through the great places of Europe, whereas mine was a straight line from Greenock to little Idvor, so little that it cannot be found on any map.

There was just one thing which delayed my straight-line journey to Idvor. A visit to Cambridge was necessary in order to arrange for my work at this university during the coming academic year, and I lost no time in reaching it. The sight of the Firth of Clyde, with its wonderfully green slopes, of Greenock, of Glasgow, and even of London made feeble impressions. My mind was centred upon one thought only: the speedy return to Idvor. This also explains why my first sight of Cambridge impressed me much less than my first sight of Princeton when, eight years before, I had enjoyed my loaf of bread under an elm-tree in front of Nassau Hall. F. Marion Crawford, the novelist, had given me a letter of introduction to Oscar Browning, a fellow of King's College; and George Rives, the late chairman of the Board of Trustees of Columbia University, had given me a letter to W. D. Niven, a fellow of Trinity College. Rives, after graduating at Columbia College, won a prize scholarship in classics at Trinity College, and gained there many scholastic honors.

The man at the ancient gate of King's College informed me that Mr. Oscar Browning was away on his summer vacation. At Trinity College I had better luck, and the man at the still more ancient gate of Trinity College took me to Mr. Niven, who reminded me much of Professor Merriam, the great Greek scholar of Columbia College; the same kindly expression of a most intelligent face, and the same gentle light from two thoughtful eyes. As I looked into his eyes I felt that I was catching a glimpse of a world full of those beautiful things which make life worth living. I informed Niven that I wished to come to Cambridge and study under Professor James Clerk Maxwell, the creator of the new electrical theory. Niven looked puzzled and asked me who had told me of this new theory, and when I mentioned Rutherfurd, he asked me what Rutherfurd had told me about it. "That it will probably give a satisfactory answer to the question: 'What is Light?'" I answered, and watched for his reaction. "Did not Mr. Rutherfurd tell you that Clerk Maxwell died four years ago?" asked Niven, and when I said no, he asked me whether I had not seen it in the preface to the second edition of Maxwell's great book which Niven himself had edited.

This question embarrassed me, and I confessed frankly that Rutherfurd's son, my chum Winthrop, had presented me with this book on the day of the sailing of my ship; that it was packed away in my bags; and that I did not have any time to examine it during the voyage, because I was too busy helping to entertain twelve beautiful schoolgirls from Washington, who were making their first trip to Europe. Niven laughed heartily and admitted, jokingly, that twelve beautiful girls from Washington were certainly more attractive than any theory, not excepting even Maxwell's great electrical theory. He suggested then that I could study at Cambridge under Lord Rayleigh, who had succeeded Maxwell as professor of physics. I declined the suggestion on the ground that I had never heard of Lord Rayleigh before. Niven laughed again, even more heartily than before, and assured me that Lord Rayleigh was a great physicist in spite of the fact that his great fame had never reached my ears. An

English lord a great physicist! The idea struck me as strange, but Niven looked so friendly and so sincere that I could not help believing that he really meant what he said. He invited me to lunch, and before we parted I assured him that I would come back to Cambridge in the following October and place myself under his guidance.

This conference with Niven sobered me up very considerably; it convinced me that my great aspiration and my small preparation in physics were far from being of the same order of magnitude. I confessed to Niven that my success in winning prizes in science at Columbia College had led to my belief that I knew more physics than I really did. "Confession is a splendid thing for the soul," said Niven, and added: "But do not permit that anything I have said dampen your courage. A physicist needs courage, and few mortals were braver than Maxwell. The world knows only a little of his great electrical theory, but it knows even less of his great moral courage." He gave me a copy of Campbell's life of Maxwell; I read it from cover to cover before I left London, and it contributed much to the learning which I had promised to bring to Idvor. It certainly convinced me that Maxwell had a vastly better knowledge of physics when he graduated at Cambridge than I had picked up at Columbia. That gave me much healthy food for serious thought.

A straight line from London to Idvor passes through Switzerland, and I proposed to follow that line in my journey as closely as practicable. My ticket took me from London to Lucerne directly; the journey from Lucerne to Idvor I left undetermined until I reached

Lucerne. I had no time nor inclination to explore the wonders of London, Paris, or of any other great place in Europe before I had seen Idvor again. Mother, Idvor, and Maxwell's new electrical theory had brought me to Europe, and I wished to see them as soon as possible, and in the order named; everything else could wait. Besides, I sincerely believed that these places had little to offer to a fellow like me, who knew the great things of New York. I was much disposed to look down upon things in Europe, a mental attitude which is not uncommon among American immigrants when they go back to pay a temporary visit to Europe. I had it quite strongly, but sobering experiences like the conference with Niven in Cambridge helped me to apply suitable correction factors to this mental attitude. The following brief description of one of these experiences bears upon this point.

The London-Lucerne train crossed the Franco-Swiss frontier very early in the morning, somewhere near Neuchâtel. The delay necessary for the rearrangement of the train gave the passengers ample time to enjoy their breakfast in the garden of the station restaurant. A look to the east caught a sight which made me almost forget my breakfast. The distant snow-covered Alps, bathed in the early sunshine and projected against the background of the luminous blue sky of a July morning, furnished a picture never to be forgotten. I had never seen the Alps before, and this first view of them was of overpowering beauty.

An Englishman, a fellow traveller, sitting opposite me at the breakfast-table, noticed my mental exaltation, and asked: "You have never seen the Alps before, have you?" "No," said I. "Oh, what a lucky lad you are!" said the Englishman, adding that he would give much to be in my place. He confessed that he had to climb the peaks of the Alps in order to get those thrills which in former days, when he was of my age, he got by looking at them from the valleys below. At his suggestion we continued our journey to Lucerne in the same compartment, and the stories of his climbing exploits stirred up mightily my imagination, which was already throbbing under the inspiration of the Alpine view which had greeted me that morning. When I informed him that I was in a hurry to reach my native village of Idvor, otherwise I might try some climbing myself, he assured me that a ten days' delay in Lucerne would suffice to prepare me for climbing one of the lesser peaks, and he mentioned Titlis, not far from Lucerne. He prescribed the training which would provide me with sufficiently steady Alpine legs. From the peak of the Titlis, he said, I could see old Switzerland where the famous legend was born which relates how Tell drove the fear of God into the hearts of the Austrians. I always loved that legend, perhaps because I did not love the Austrian tyrants. When the train had reached Lucerne I saw the wonderful Alpine panorama spread out like an amphitheatre of snow-covered Alpine peaks around its deep-blue lake, and I knew that in spite of my great haste to reach Idvor I would not leave this fairy-land before I had reached the snow-covered peak of Titlis.

I immediately hired a rowboat for a week, and, clad in a rowing shirt with blue and white Columbia stripes and thin tennis trousers, I spent that afternoon exploring the beauty spots of the meandering shore of the historic lake. The joy of rowing and the busy rays of the July sun made me yield to the invitation of the clear waters of the lake to plunge in and hug the waves, which once upon a time carried Tell to safety after he had sent his arrow through the heart of the Austrian tyrant, Gessler. As if imitating the example of Tell, I jumped in just as I was, trusting that subsequent rowing and the sun would dry my scanty attire, and they did. A glorious feeling of freedom from all earthly restraints came over me as, floating on my back, I beheld the blue sky above and the snow-covered peaks around me. It was the same sky and the same luminous peaks, I thought, which five hundred years before saw William Tell chase away the Austrian tyrants from the historic cantons surrounding the lake; from Uri, Schwyz, and Unterwalden. I felt that I was floating in the very cradle where real freedom first saw the light of day. No other spot on earth was more worthy of that immortal fame. My admiration for it never faded after that memorable July afternoon. Europe rose in my estimation; I was much less inclined to look down upon things European.

The next day I was up very early, feeling "as a strong man ready to run a race," the same feeling which I had experienced at Castle Garden when, nine years before, I woke up early in the morning and hurried off to catch my first glimpse of the great American metropolis. I was just as anxious to hurry off and catch from some mountain-top my first glimpse of Switzerland. Mindful of the suggestions of my English acquaintance on the train, I started with the easiest climb, the Rigi

Culm. It is a very easy effort, but I made it difficult by rowing first some ten miles to Weggis, going up to the Rigi and walking down, and then rowing back to Lucerne again on the same day, in the waning hours of the afternoon. An unexpected squall upset my boat, and I had quite a struggle to get back to Lucerne, very late in the evening. The hotel proprietor noticed my mussed-up appearance, but said nothing, seeing that I was not in a communicative mood.

The same strenuous method of preparatory training for the Titlis climb took me up to Mount Pilatus on the next day. But I was not allowed to return on the same day on account of a fierce thunder-storm raging in the valley below, which I watched from the top of the Pilatus. The innkeeper congratulated me upon my rare luck, not only because I had a chance to see the beautiful sight of a thunder-storm as viewed from a point above the thundering clouds, but principally because this thunder-storm prevented me from running the serious risk of descending and rowing back to Lucerne on the same day. Commenting upon the over-confidence of youth, the innkeeper said that every person has a guardian angel, but people intoxicated by wine or by exuberance of youth have two, one on each side. That was his explanation for the alleged fact, he said, that young people and intoxicated people seldom meet with serious accidents in mountain climbing. Some Americans, he thought, should have several guardian angels. This sarcasm was aimed at me, and it did not miss its mark.

Nevertheless, when on my fifth day in Lucerne I started out very early for the Titlis, I adopted the same strenuous method: rowing to Stansstadt, walking to Engelberg, and climbing to the hospice where I arrived at 11 P.M. I reached at sunrise of the following morning the top of Titlis, and saw the glories of Uri, Schwyz, and Unterwalden as my English friend had promised. But I reached it much exhausted, and if it had not been for the skilled assistance of my trusty Swiss guide, the last four lines of Longfellow's "Excelsior" would have described my Titlis climb quite accurately. I quote the lines:

> "There in the twilight cold and gray,
> Lifeless, but beautiful, he lay,
> And from the sky, serene and far,
> A voice fell, like a falling star,
> Excelsior!"

Returning from Titlis, I ran into my English friend, and he remarked that I looked a little overtrained. We dined together, and when I told him the story of my six days' Alpine experience, he begged me to hustle off to Idvor and see my mother first, and then return if I cared to pursue my own methods of exploring the beauties of Switzerland. "If you continue pursuing these methods now, I am afraid that your mother will never see you again, because there are not enough guardian angels in all the heavens to prevent you from breaking your neck." I agreed, but assured him that my overstrenuous method of climbing Titlis was worth the risk; it had humbled my vanity and false pride, and made me more respectful to some of the slow ways of old Europe. It convinced me that even after serving my apprenticeship as greenhorn in the United States,

I could still be a most verdant greenhorn in Europe. The railroad journey from Lucerne to Vienna afforded me much leisure time for philosophic reflections upon this matter. Thanks to Niven in Cambridge and to my English friend in Lucerne, I reached Vienna with a mental attitude considerably different from and certainly much less exalted than that which I had taken along when I sailed from New York four weeks before.

The railroad-station at Vienna where I took the train for Budapest looked quite familiar, although I had seen it but once before. I did not discover the great and mighty station-master who at my first appearance there, eleven years before, nearly sent me back to the prisons of the military frontier. The conductor, however, who called me "Gnaediger Herr" (gracious sir), when near Gaenserndorf he asked me for my first-class ticket, was the same man who, eleven years before, had called me a Serbian swineherd. I recognized him easily, although he looked very humble and had lost the fierceness which he had displayed when he roughly pulled me off my seat on that memorable first railroad journey from Budapest to Vienna. He failed to recall to memory the Serbian boy with yellow sheepskin coat and cap and the gaily colored bag. I gave him a generous tip as a reward for driving me into the arms of my good American friends who had seen me safely landed in Prague, and the memory of whose kind act had suggested my running off to the land of Lincoln.

"America is the land of rapid changes," he said, when I told him that I was that boy, and he added: "You must have changed much, looking as you do like

a real American; but we here and our dear old Austria
are like all old people; we do not change except to
grow older and more decrepit." He expressed exactly
what I felt as I looked to the right and to the left of
the train which was taking me to Budapest. Everything seemed to move slowly, with the deliberate step
of feeble old age. Budapest looked small, and the suspension bridge, which had nearly taken my breath
away eleven years before, when I first saw it, looked
puny in comparison with the Brooklyn suspension
bridge.

I spent no time in looking around to explore the vir-
tues of the Magyar metropolis, but hustled, and presently I was on the boat which eleven years before had
brought me to Budapest. I could hardly believe that
it was the same boat. It must have shrunk incredibly,
I thought, or else my life in America had changed the
vision of my eyes. Everything I saw looked small and
shrivelled up, and if I had not seen the snow-covered
giants of Switzerland as viewed from the top of Titlis,
Europe itself might have appeared to me as small and
shrivelled up.

When supper was served I noticed that everybody
had atrocious table manners, even people of high official
rank, several of whom I discovered among my fellow
passengers. Eleven years before everybody on the boat
had looked so high and mighty that I was almost afraid
to look at them, but this time I was much tempted to
imagine that I was considerably above most of my fellow passengers. I resisted the temptation. It was a
good thing that my climbing of the Titlis had nearly
floored me; it suppressed much of that haughtiness

which naturalized American immigrants bring with them when they visit Europe.

The next morning I noticed a group of Serb students who were returning home from the universities of Vienna and Budapest. They were from my native Voyvodina, and not from Serbia, as I found out later. Their appearance did not impress me very agreeably, but nevertheless I quivered with delight when I heard their Serb language. They spoke freely, although they must have noticed that they attracted my attention. One of them remarked that I could pass for a Serb, if it were not for my manner, my dress, and my very ruddy complexion. The voyage across the Atlantic and a week's tramping in Switzerland were responsible for my exaggerated ruddiness. A second one thought that young Serb peasants in Banat are just as ruddy, particularly during the harvest season, but he admitted that my appearance did not suggest that my occupation was that of a peasant.

Another one suggested that I was probably a rich South American with very much red Indian blood in my veins. I laughed and, introducing myself, informed him, speaking Serb with some difficulty, that I was neither a South American nor an Indian, but just a Serb student who was a citizen of the United States. A Serb from the United States was a very rare bird in those days and, needless to say, I was invited most cordially to join the group, which I did. Not one of them reminded me of the alert, well-groomed, athletic, and playful American college boys. They all had long hair brushed back in a careless fashion, affecting the appearance of dreamy poets or disciples of radical doctrines. Most of them had slouch hats with wide brims, indicating radical tendencies. Their faces looked pale and suggested excessive indoor confinement in Vienna and Budapest cafés, playing chess or cards, or discussing radical doctrines.

Most of them would have been hazed if they had matriculated in any American college without modifying much their appearance and manner. They certainly took themselves very seriously. They knew, I thought, many things which they had read in books, principally in books dealing with radical social-science theories. Tolstoy's name was mentioned quite often, and the latest apostles of socialistic doctrines also had their share of adulation. They must have observed that conversation about these things bored me, and they asked me, with some display of sarcasm, I thought, whether American college students took any interest in modern advanced thought. "They do," said I, considerably irritated, "and if it were not for Maxwell's new electrical theory and for other advanced theories in modern physics I should not have come to your moribund old Europe." "Advanced thought in social and not in physical sciences," they said, explaining their original question, and I answered that the most popular American doctrine in social science still rested upon foundations laid a hundred years before that time, in a document called the Declaration of Independence. They knew very little about it, and I knew even less about their radical social-science theories, and we changed the subject of our conversation.

Late in the afternoon the boat approached Karlovci

and the hills of Frushka Gora. I could not help remi-
niscing, and entertained my Serb acquaintances with a
description of my experiences with the theological students eleven years before, including the disappearance
of my roast goose. My Serbian vocabulary was quite
shaky, but nevertheless I made quite a hit, and they
begged me to go on with my reminiscences. Whenever
I was at a loss for a word, they helped me out. Toward
sunset Belgrade hove in sight, and its majestic appearance thrilled me and made my Serb vocabulary run as
smoothly as ever. I saluted Belgrade as the acropolis
of all the Serbs, and expressed the hope that it might
soon become the metropolis of all the southern Slavs.
"This is the kind of advanced thought in social and
political science that American students are interested
in," I said, reminding them of their former question,
and I added a few sarcastic remarks about advanced
thoughts in social and political science which are not
born in the heart of a nation but imported from the
dens of French, German, and Russian theorists. They
quickly caught what I called the American point of
view, but they did not oppose it, for fear, I thought, of
offending me. They saw the American chip on my
shoulder, and did not care to knock it off.

I had not seen Belgrade since I was a little boy, and
as the boat approached it I saw its high fort rising like a
Gibraltar above the waters of the Danube and looking
anxiously across the endless plains of Austria-Hungary,
which, like wide-open jaws of a hungry dragon, seemed
to threaten to swallow it up. Everything I saw in Austria-Hungary looked small and shrivelled up, but Belgrade looked to me as if its proud head would touch

the stars. The history of the long-suffering Serb race was grouped around it, and that lifted it up in my imagination to sublime heights. I was much tempted to stop there and climb up to the top of Mount Avala, near Belgrade, and from there send my greetings to heroic Serbia, just as I had sent my greetings to heroic Switzerland from the top of snow-covered Titlis. But I was told to look sharp if I wished to catch the last local boat to Panchevo, and so I bade good-by and au revoir to white-towered Belgrade, as the Serbian guslars call it.

When the local boat arrived in Panchevo a delegation of young men, including one of the Serb students who had come with me from Budapest, transferred me to another boat, which was crowded with what looked like a gay wedding-party. The singing society of Panchevo had chartered this boat to take it and its friends to Karlovci, where a great national gathering of Serbs was to take place on the following day. The earthly remains of the great Serb poet Branko Radichevich were to arrive there from Vienna, where, when still a youth, he died and had been buried thirty years before. His body was to be transferred to and buried near Karlovci, on Strazhilovo hill, which was glorified by his immortal verses. His lyrics were messages to all Serbs, calling upon them to nurse their traditions and prepare for their national reunion. Representative Serbs from all parts of Serbdom were to assemble in Karlovci to escort the earthly remains of the popular poet to his last resting-place. I was to represent America, hence the invitation to join the Panchevo delegation. Serb nationalism flamed up in my heart again.

Our boat arrived at Karlovci in the early hours of the
following morning, and there we found many singing
societies and delegates from Voyvodina, Serbia, Bosnia,
Hercegovina, and Montenegro—a most picturesque
gathering of splendid-looking young men and women,
many of them in their national costumes of brilliant
colors. The funeral procession started early in the afternoon. The singing societies from the principal cen-
tres of Serbdom, lined up in the march in proper succession, took up in turn the singing of the solemn
and wonderfully harmonious funeral hymn: "Holy
God, almighty God, immortal God, have mercy upon
us."

The Orthodox church permits no instrumental music.
Those who have had the good fortune to listen to Russian choirs know the power and the spiritual charm of
their choral singing. Serb choirs are not their inferiors.
No music appeals to our hearts so strongly as the music
of the human voice. Every one of the singers in that
procession at Karlovci felt that he was paying his last
vocal tribute to the sacred memory of the national
poet, and his voice rose up to the heavens above as if
carried there by the wings of his inspired soul. The
effect was irresistible, and there was not a single dry
eye in the great national gathering. A dismembered
nation united in tears was a most solemn and inspiring
spectacle. One could not help feeling that these tears
were welcome to the thirsty soil which nourished the
roots of Serb nationalism. A nation which is united in
song and in tears will never lose its unity. If the governments of Vienna and Budapest had foreseen the
emotions which that solemn ceremony would arouse in

the hearts of that vast and representative gathering coming from every part of the dismembered Serbdom, they would never have permitted it. But that would have meant the exercise of the perceptions of subtle psychology, which these governments never had.

When the boat returned to Panchevo, Protoyeray Zhivkovich, the poet-priest, who had first suggested my transference from Panchevo to Prague, was watching for my arrival, and received me with tears of joy in his eyes. He was a protecting friend and adviser of my boyhood days, and he always considered himself indirectly responsible for my wandering away to the distant shores of America. When I thanked him for the choice feast which he had prepared for me, he assured me that his feast was only a feast of food, whereas the feast which I spread out before him when I answered his questions about America was a feast for his soul. I certainly did it, if I interpreted correctly the luminous flashes of his intelligent eyes. He was a man of about sixty, but his vigorous eye was still just as eloquent as the stirring verses of his younger days. "Tell your mother," he said, "that I am happy to bear the whole responsibility for your wandering away to distant America. It is no longer distant; it is now in my heart; you have brought America to us. It was a new world in my terrestrial geography; it is now a new world in my spiritual geography." His generous enthusiasm threatened to undo some of the sobering effects of Niven's conference at Cambridge. During my several visits at his house that summer I had to repeat again and again my description of Beecher and of his sermons. He called him the brother of Joan of Arc of the new spiritual world; her flaming sword, he said, was "Uncle Tom's Cabin."

My older sister and her husband drove to Panchevo and escorted me to Idvor. When Idvor's territory was reached I begged them to make a detour which would take me through the pasturelands and vineyards of Idvor, where I had seen my happiest boyhood days. There, as if in a dream, I saw the boys of Idvor watching herds of oxen just as I used to do, and playing the same games which I used to play. The vineyards, the summer sky above them, and the river Tamish in the distance, where I had learned to swim and dive, looked the same as ever. Presently the familiar church-spire of Idvor hove in sight, and gradually the sweet sound of the church-bells, announcing vespers, awakened countless memories in my mind and I found it difficult to control my emotions. As we drove slowly through little Idvor everything looked exactly as it had looked eleven years before. There were no new houses, and the old ones looked as old as ever. The people were doing the same work which they always did during that season of the year, and they were doing it in the same way.

When we reached the village green I saw the gate of my mother's yard wide open, a sign that she expected a welcome guest. She sat alone on the bench under a tree in front of her house, and waited, looking in the direction from which she expected me to come. When she saw my sister's team, I observed that suddenly she raised her white handkerchief to her eyes, and my sister whispered to me: "Mayka plache!" ("Mother is weeping!") I jumped out of the wagon and hastened to embrace her. Oh, how wonderful is the power of tears, and how clear is our spiritual vision when a shower of tears has purified the turbulent atmosphere of our emotions! Mother's love and love for mother are the sweetest messages of God to the living earth.

Everything in Idvor looked the same, but my mother had changed; she looked much older, and much more beautiful. There was a saintly light in her eyes which disclosed to me the serene firmament of the spiritual world in which she lived. Raphael and Titian, I thought, never painted a more beautiful saint. I gazed and worshipped and felt most humble. "Come," she said, "and walk with me; we shall be alone; I want to hear your voice and see the light of your face, undisturbed." We walked slowly, and my mother recalled many things, reminding me of the familiar objects of my boyhood days, as: "Here is the path on which you walked to school; there is the church where you read the epistles on Sundays and holidays; there is the mill with the funnel-shaped thatched roof from the top of which you once removed the shining new tin star, imagining that it was a star from heaven; there is the house where Baba Batikin, of blessed memory, lived and taught you so many ancient tales; there is the house where old Aunt Tina cured your whooping-cough with charms and with herbs steeped in honey; here lived old Lyubomir, of blessed memory, who was so fond of you, and made your sheepskin coats and caps; here is the field where every evening you brought our horses to the chikosh (the village herdsman) to take them to the pasturelands."

OLYMPIADA PUPIN, MOTHER OF MICHAEL PUPIN
From a photograph taken in 1880

By that time we had reached the end of the little village, but my mother prolonged our leisurely walk and presently we stood at the gate of the village cemetery. Pointing to a cross of red marble my mother said that it marked the grave of my father. When we reached it I kissed the cross, and, kneeling upon the grave, I prayed. My mother, loyal to Serb traditions, addressed the grave, saying: "Kosta, my faithful husband, here is your boy whom you loved more dearly than your own life, and whose name was on your lips when you breathed your last. Accept his prayer and his tears as his affectionate tribute to your blessed memory, which he will cherish forever."

On the way back we stopped at the church and kissed the icons of our patron saint and of St. Sava, and lighted two wax candles which mother had brought with her. I confessed to her that I felt as if a sacred communion had reunited me with the spirit of Idvor. That was her wish, she said, because she did not want Idvor to think that I was like a proud stranger from a proud, strange land. "I did not recognize you," she said, "when I first saw you in your sister's wagon until you smiled with the smile of your boyhood days, and then I shed the sweetest tears of my life. You looked so learned and so far above us plain folks of Idvor that nobody will recognize the Misha they used to know, and whom they long to see, unless you show them the boy that they used to know." My promise to return to Idvor "rich in learning and academic honors" was evidently made good, according to my mother's opinion. But did not this learning and these academic honors carry with them an air which did not harmonize with the old-fashioned notions of Idvor? This, I believed, was in my mother's mind, and I made a careful note of it.

Idvor came to see me, and it assured me that there was no youngster in all the great plains of Voyvodina who was nearer to the heart of his native village than Misha. This affectionate regard was won by my strict observance of all the old customs of Idvor, as, for instance, kissing the hand of the old people of Idvor, and in return being kissed by them on the forehead. On the other hand, young peasant boys and girls of Idvor kissed my hand, and I kissed them on the cheek and petted them. My cousin, much older than I, was an ex-soldier and a stern *Knez* (chief) of the village. He was the oldest male member and, therefore, the head of the Pupins. I was expected to keep this in mind constantly, and I did it whenever I stood in his mighty presence. American citizenship eliminated my allegiance to the Emperor of Austria-Hungary but not to the autocratic *Knez* of Idvor.

There was another great person in Idvor whose presence inspired awe. He was my *koum* (godfather). My mother had lost all her children that were born in her earlier years, and was left childless for many years. She then bore two daughters when she was over thirty. I was born when she was over forty, in answer to her fervent prayer, she firmly believed, that God grant her a son. A boy born late in life, if he is to live, must, according to a popular belief in Idvor, be handed out through the front window to the first person who comes along, and that person has to carry the baby to church quickly and have it baptized. In this manner a very poor and humble peasant of Idvor became my *koum*. A *koum's* authority over his godchild is, theoretically at least, unlimited, according to Serbian custom. In practice, a godchild must eat humble pie when the *koum* is present. Between my cousin, who, as *Knez*, was at the head of the village, and my *koum*, who was somewhere near the bottom of the village, I had some difficulty to steer the correct course of conduct. I succeeded, thanks to my efforts to please my mother; and the peasants of Idvor most cheerfully admitted that America must be a fine Christian country, since it had given me a training which harmonized so well with the Christian traditions of Idvor. My presidency in the junior year at Columbia College, my undisputed authority among some of the young aristocrats of New York, and the many scholastic successes in my academic career had sown some seeds of vanity and false pride in my heart. But these seeds were smothered by the inexorable rigors of Idvor's traditions. Humility is the cardinal virtue in a youth among the peasants of Idvor.

Needless to say, the story of my life since I had left Idvor was retold many a time, until my mother and my sisters knew it by heart. It was sweet music to their ears. I enjoyed it, too, because summer evenings in a Serbian garden are most conducive to the spinning out of reminiscent tales. The village worthies spent many Sunday afternoons in my mother's garden asking many, many a question about America. Tales about things like the Brooklyn Bridge, the elevated railroads, the tall buildings in New York, and the agricultural operations of the West were received with many expressions of wonder, but at times also, I thought, with some reserve. A simple peasant mind could not accept without considerable reserve the statement that a machine can cut, bind, and load the seasoned wheat, all at the same time, with nothing but a few stupid horses to drag it along. After a while my store of information became exhausted, and I had much less to say, but the wise men of Idvor urged me to go on. They met my apologies with the statement that peasant Ghiga had never left Idvor in all his life until one day he went to a neighboring village, about ten miles away, and saw the county fair. He returned to Idvor on the same day, and for six weeks he never ceased talking about the great things which he had seen at that county fair. "Just imagine," said the priest, "how much he would have had to say if he had been nine years in great America!"

## EDITORIAL NOTE

THE summer in Idvor passed quickly with fêtes for the visitor. At times he felt a vague homesick yearning for the simple pleasures of his native village. But his mother's "The real things are waiting for you at Cambridge" was the only spur needed to revive his enthusiasm for his studies. At Cambridge he adapted himself to the university routine—work in the morning and evening and play in the afternoon. Mr. Pupin's work was with the honor group in mathematics and his play rowing in the college boat. Before him was always the problem "What is light?" James Clerk Maxwell had written a great electrical treatise in an attempt to answer that question, and into this work and the writings of Michael Faraday, Mr. Pupin delved, reading and re-reading, satisfied only with complete understanding. His mother had said, "Cambridge is a great temple consecrated to the *eternal truth;* it is filled with icons of the great saints of science. The contemplation of their saintly work will enable you to communicate with the spirit of *eternal truth.*"

Mr. Pupin went that summer to Pornic, on the coast of France, where he read the *Life of Maxwell* and learned to speak French, so that, when he found in a second-hand bookshop a copy of La Grange's *Méchanique Analytique,* he was able to master it in the original language. The remaining weeks of the holiday were spent with his mother in Idvor.

Back at Cambridge, Michael Pupin completed his work with satisfaction, but he still felt the lack of the "knowledge of visible things—acquired by the learner's own conscious efforts." So after a summer in Scotland, the land of Maxwell, Mr. Pupin transferred to the University of Berlin where his work in experimental physics under Professor von Helmholtz might bring him closer to this "knowledge."

It was during the following winter that Mr. Pupin's mother died. Twenty-seven years later it was possible for him to found in her memory a scholarship to assist poor schoolboys of Old Serbia and Macedonia.

After his marriage in London to Miss Jackson, an American, Mr. and Mrs. Pupin returned to New York where he took up his work as "Teacher of Mathematical Physics in the Department of Electrical Engineering in the School of Mines of Columbia College." The title was impressive, but the building for the new department was a small brick shed, called by the students the "cowshed." Here with very limited laboratory facilities Mr. Pupin did much important research work, and perfected his electrical resonators which have played so large a part in bringing about radio broadcasting. He also invented here his mathematical theory of long-distance telephony and with its aid constructed the first long-distance telephone cable. Such cables are universally employed today.

When the X-rays were discovered in Germany, Mr. Pupin's previous experience made it possible for him to repeat Roentgen's experiments and to obtain the first X-ray photograph ever made in America. This brought to his laboratory doctors with crippled patients, hoping that X-ray photographs might suggest a cure by showing where the trouble lay. A famous surgeon sent a man with nearly a hundred small shot in his hand. At this time an exposure of nearly an hour would have been necessary in order to obtain a satisfactory photograph. By a combination of a fluorescent screen and a photographic plate Mr. Pupin was able to obtain in a few seconds a photograph which showed every shot and made possible the first surgical operation in America under guidance of an X-ray picture. This is the method of X-ray photography practised everywhere today.

On April 14, 1896, Mr. Pupin finished writing out a full report of his X-ray researches. He looked back over his six years at Columbia with a feeling of keen satisfaction in work well done. The very next day a severe chill was the forerunner of an attack of pneumonia which almost took Mr. Pupin's life. When he was strong enough to be told that his wife had died during his illness, that terrible news shattered his nerves, and only the fact that he had a little daughter to bring up gave him an interest in living. At his doctor's suggestion he went for the summer to Norfolk, Connecticut, and there he now spends the summer vacation on his farm.

Mr. Pupin has become an important part of the life of his adopted country. He was influential in the founding of the American Physical Society and of the National Research Council which was established during the World War. He has used the knowledge brought from the plains of his native Idvor and that acquired by reading and study of great scientists, added much hard work and initiative of his own to create something which the world has recognized and which people now accept as essential in their daily lives.